LANGUAGE ARTS
Detecting and Correcting Special Needs

Joyce S. Choate/*Consulting Editor*

THOMAS A. RAKES
Memphis State University

JOYCE S. CHOATE
Northeast Louisiana University

ALLYN AND BACON, INC.
Boston / London / Sydney / Toronto

THE ALLYN AND BACON
DETECTING AND CORRECTING SERIES
Joyce S. Choate, *Consulting Editor*

Copyright © 1989 by Allyn and Bacon, Inc.
A Division of Simon & Schuster
160 Gould Street
Needham Heights, MA 02194-2310

Editorial-Production Service: Karen G. Mason
Copyeditor: Susan Freese
Cover Administrator: Linda K. Dickinson
Cover Designer: Susan Slovinsky

Library of Congress Cataloging-in-Publication Data

Rakes, Thomas A.
    Language arts, detecting and correcting special needs / Thomas A.
Rakes, Joyce S. Choate.
    p.   cm.   — (The Allyn and Bacon detecting and correcting series)
    Includes index.
    ISBN 0-205-11636-1
    1. Handicapped children— Education— Language arts. I. Choate,
Joyce S. II. Title. III. Series.
LC4028.R34 1988
371.9'044—dc19   88-10178
                                          CIP

Printed in the United States of America

10 9 8 7 6 5 4 3 2 1   93 92 91 90 89 88

Contents

Foreword

ABOUT THE *DETECTING AND CORRECTING SERIES*

Language Arts: Detecting and Correcting Special Needs is one of several books in an affordable series that focuses on the classroom needs of special students, both exceptional and nonexceptional, who often require adjusted methods and curricula. The purpose of this book, as well as the others, is to supplement more comprehensive and theoretical treatments of major instructional issues—in this case, teaching language arts—with practical classroom practices.

The underlying theme of each book in the *Allyn and Bacon Detecting and Correcting Series* is targeted instruction to maximize students' progress in school. Designed for informed teachers and teachers-in-training who are responsible for instructing special students in a variety of settings, these books emphasize the application of theory to everyday classroom concerns. While this approach may not be unique, the format in which both theme and purpose are presented is, in that it enables the reader to quickly translate theory into practical classroom strategies for reaching hard-to-teach students.

Each book begins with an overview of instruction in the given subject, addressing in particular the needs of special students. The groundwork is laid here for both Detection and Correction—observing students' difficulties and then designing an individualized prescriptive program. Remaining chapters are organized into sequentially numbered units, addressing specific skill needs of special students. Each unit follows a consistent two-part format. Detection is addressed first, beginning with a citation of a few significant behaviors and continuing with a discussion of factors such as descriptions and implications. The second part of each unit is Correction, where a number of principles or strategies are offered for modification according to students' learning needs.

This simple, consistent format makes the *Detecting and Correcting* books accessible and easy to read. Other useful features include: a) the Contents organization designed for quick location of problem skills and behaviors; b) cross-references among units; c) a "Reflections" section ending each part, providing discussion and application activities; and d) an index of general topics and cross-references to related subjects.

Along with the topics of related books—reading, basic mathematics, and classroom behavior—language arts represents a major area in which special students often require special accommodations. Together, these books comprise the first installment of what is envisioned to be a larger series that simplifies teachers' tasks by offering sound and practical classroom procedures for detecting and correcting special needs

Joyce S. Choate
Consulting Editor

Preface

Language Arts: Detecting and Correcting Special Needs is designed to address the language needs of special students. It is intended for use as a field resource and supplementary text by teachers and prospective teachers who are concerned with improving the language arts skills of special learners in both regular and special education classroom settings. A practical complement to theoretical texts and teaching wisdom, this book is deliberately brief and concise. The intent is to enable the reader to quickly translate the theories of language arts and special education into practical classroom strategies to improve the language arts skills of special students.

ASSUMPTIONS

In this text, special students include both properly identified exceptional learners and nonexceptional learners who demonstrate particular problems in the language arts. The basic assumptions underlying the structure and content of the book are these:

- Because the language arts are interrelated, instruction in one area supplements and reinforces skills in the other areas.
- Special students are likely to have special language arts instructional needs that may vary from those of the typical classroom student who makes average progress.
- The generally accepted sequence of the language arts skills, progressing from listening to speaking and then to reading and writing, may not apply to some special students.
- Many of the language arts needs of special students may be detected by observing and analyzing their performances of a variety of classroom tasks.
- To correct the language arts problems of special learners, it is appropriate to provide direct instruction in how to accomplish manageable tasks and then apply the tasks in a meaningful language context.
- A skill-specific corrective program for language arts can be effective with special populations and can also be incorporated into other lessons.

These assumptions are incorporated into the detection and correction model for identifying the special skill needs of individual students and then correcting those needs with targeted instruction in the language arts.

ORGANIZATION

The Contents is designed to provide a specific, at-a-glance guide to quickly locate the language arts needs of special students. For ease of reference and discussion, categories of special students and specific language skills are enumerated and often treated as intact units. Although labeled as discrete segments, it is important to remember that in the real world, neither student behaviors nor language skills operate according to such tidy classifications.

The text is divided into five major parts. Each part begins with an overview and concludes with suggestions for reflecting on the content. "Reflections" are intended for clarification, discussion, extension, and application. In each part, the final "Reflections" item refers to additional resources for further information.

The three chapters in Part I describe special language arts instruction and special students. The first chapter briefly explains the validated teaching practices that form the foundation for what we consider to be special instruction in the language arts. These teaching practices provide the framework for the corrective strategies for each of the language skill needs in later chapters. The next two chapters outline categories of special students, both exceptional and nonexceptional, and offer a few general guidelines for designing corrective programs for each group.

Listening skills are described in the three chapters of Part II. These auditory attention, comprehension, memory, and appreciation skills facilitate the acquisition of language and learning in the classroom. Part III focuses on speaking skills. In these two chapters, both types and formats of oral expression as well as special speech problems are discussed. The traditional reading topics—word recognition, reading comprehension, and study skills—are considered in Part IV. To emphasize their respective contributions to the writing process, the chapters in Part V begin with written expression. Following the focus on the generation and expression of ideas, written grammar skills are presented as the mechanics for clarifying written ideas. This chapter concludes with the application of grammar and mechanics to written expression in the final step of the writing process, revising and editing. In the remaining two chapters, spelling and handwriting are depicted as supplementary writing skills.

FEATURES

These detecting and correcting strategies are grounded in theory but shaped by practitioners. Their uniqueness resides in their practicality and versatility. Most of them can be implemented in both regular and special education classrooms with individual, small groups, and even large groups of students. Because the strategies must be adapted to fit individual students and teachers, only the most salient features are described. To keep the text clear, succinct, and practical, theories of language arts and special education are built into the strategies.

As a study and reference aid, a consistent format is used throughout. Every chapter includes a diagnostic section entitled DETECTION and a prescriptive teaching section entitled CORRECTION. In the first chapter, the two sections contain a quick look at common diagnostic practices in the language arts and several teaching practices that apply to correction.

Chapters Two and Three describe a number of groups of special learners. For each group, DETECTION consists of a list of a few general behaviors, followed by a description of the types of language difficulties likely to occur, possible explanations of the problems, and the implications of the language needs to academic progress. The CORRECTION component offers basic principles as corrective guidelines. With the exception of the generic special education category, each group is described on a single page.

In Chapters 4 through 15, the discussion of the detection and correction of each language skill is expanded to two facing pages. Each treatment begins with a list of a few behaviors that may signal a special need for instruction in the particular language arts skill. Related skills are referenced by skill numbers in parentheses. Next is a description of the skill and of the problems students often exhibit. The possible causes for skill weakness and the implications for achievement, other subjects, and instruction are mentioned. Strategies are suggested for correcting the skill need so that it no longer interferes with academic progress. At least five corrective strategies are described for each skill, followed by ideas for providing extra practice. Related skills from which additional corrective strategies may be adapted are listed. Many of these corrective strategies are also appropriate for most students, but it is the special student who must have the special instruction in the language arts to progress.

ACKNOWLEDGEMENTS

Reflected in these strategies are the modifications of the many teachers and students who field-tested and improved them. We appreciate the time, effort, and expertise of these practitioners, our harshest critics. For their guidance in refining the text we are grateful to our field reviewers: Susan Evans (Pensacola Junior College); Nancy Mangialetti (Union-Endicott School District, New York); and Walter Petty.

A special thank you is due our truly exceptional editorial team at Allyn and Bacon for detecting and correcting our own special needs: Mylan Jaixen, director and counselor; Ray Short, expediter; Elizabeth Brooks, facilitator; Sue Freese, groomer; and Karen Mason, engineer. And to our families and colleagues who generously tolerate and support our endeavors, we are indebted.

PART I

SPECIAL LANGUAGE ARTS NEEDS OF SPECIAL LEARNERS

The language arts are the substance of academic curricula. As core curricular subjects, reading and written expression represent two of the major areas by which academic progress is gauged. Skills in these two areas also facilitate the acquisition and demonstration of knowledge in all other subjects. Listening and speaking, although not considered to be content subjects themselves, are also primary vehicles for learning and expressing knowledge throughout all the subject areas.

All students occasionally need specific instruction to meet their individual needs in the language arts. Some students, however, require more specialized instruction than others. In this section, we briefly outline the foundation of special instruction in the language arts as well as some of the special problems that certain categories of students experience in attempting to master the language arts skills. Whether their difficulties result from learning differences, experience differences, or poor teaching, many of the students in each category share common instructional needs.

The first chapter contains several recommendations for designing special instruction in the language arts. We suggest analyzing classroom performances as the major method for detecting the language skills that need correcting. The 13 instructional practices that form the framework for our CORRECTION strategies throughout this book are described and then followed by the supporting references.

Chapter 2 focuses on the language arts difficulties frequently experienced by students in regular and remedial education class placement. The patterns of performance often described by the teachers of these classes are grouped and discussed according to similar features. Some are associated with learning problems, while others are related to the types of experiences students have or have not had.

In Chapter 3, we present some of the more common language arts problems experienced by exceptional students. Beginning with needs and CORRECTIVE PRINCIPLES that apply to several exceptionalities, we briefly survey by classification the special needs generally associated with categories of special education students. Many of these students are also taught in the regular or remedial classroom, but at least a portion of their instruction is under the direction of special educators.

Although entire books have been written on each of the special categories, we limit each discussion to the boundaries of a single page. Each page begins with a list of language behaviors often associated with the particular classification, followed by a cursory description of some typical performances, the relationship of the learning or experience problem to language difficulties, and the implications for academic progress. All students occasionally evidence some of the DETECTION behaviors. Not every student with language arts problems fits neatly into a category, nor does every classified student exhibit every problem. The DETECTION behaviors offer clues to a *possible* pattern of language arts needs. To identify and confirm exact problems, these clues must be considered along with a student's past and sustained performance and the results of evaluations by appropriate experts.

Many of the same strategies are appropriate for teaching the language arts to most students. However, to correct skill deficits, these strategies may have to be adjusted and tailored to the specific learning needs of individual students. Appropriate specialists should be consulted in all cases. The CORRECTIVE PRINCIPLES listed are ones that apply to the most typical characteristics of each category. A thorough diagnosis and analysis of each student's skills and the evaluation of targeted teaching are necessary to confirm the applicability of any principle to a specific student. These principles are intended as preliminary guides for your selection and modification of the CORRECTION strategies presented in later sections.

Note: Because of the interrelatedness of reading and the language arts, portions of the content of Part I also appear in Part I of *Reading: Detecting and Correcting Special Needs* , by J. S. Choate and T. A. Rakes (Boston: Allyn and Bacon, 1989).

Special instruction in the language arts is designed to meet the learning needs of individual special students. Such teaching involves first detecting a student's learning and skill needs and then planning instruction that will improve or correct the weaker skills so that they no longer represent a special skill need.

DETECTION

The identification of the errors to be corrected is central to any targeted instructional plan. Three ways to identify or detect the specific language arts skills in need of correction are: 1) through direct testing, using either formal or informal measures; 2) by analysis of daily classroom language interactions and behaviors; and 3) by synthesis of the data from a combination of testing and analysis of language performance in the classroom.

Direct Testing

Tests of some of the language arts skills form a major part of most group-administered standardized achievement test batteries. Typically sampled are vocabulary knowledge, silent reading comprehension, spelling skills, and knowledge of grammar and mechanics. Listening comprehension is occasionally tested, but speaking skills are not. Results of these tests are useful for making general comparisons of students' performance on a regional or national basis and for identifying students in need of a more thorough diagnosis.

Individually administered standardized tests of language arts skills are a typical part of the educational evaluation of students who are suspected of being handicapped. Results of these tests usually yield a profile of achievement of major reading and some writing skills and, when specifically assessed, oral language reception and expression. Because of the nature of the language skills and the need for their frequent and varied usage in learning activities, the formal measures often sample only a small part of a student's typical classroom language behaviors.

A number of informal testing formats are also used to diagnose language skills. Perhaps the two most popular of these tests are the widely used informal reading inventory (IRI) for assessing oral and silent reading, as well as listening comprehension skills, and the analysis of oral and written language samples. The primary classroom use of these and other informal testing techniques is to initiate plans for instruction in reading and in writing.

Analysis of Classroom Language Behaviors

Unlike direct testing, which takes time from instruction to administer the measures, the analysis of daily classroom language behaviors can occur quite naturally during almost any lesson. Instead of incomplete and single sample tests, the ongoing process of observations and the analysis of students' classroom language performance provide continuous diagnostic data to identify skill needs, monitor the effectiveness of instructional strategies, and measure language progress. In this book, we recommend direct testing to survey language skills and for more global evaluations of progress, but we emphasize the use of observable classroom language behaviors to detect the skill needs for corrective instruction in the language arts.

CORRECTION

Students with special needs are described in the next two chapters. These students require instruction in most of the same language arts skills that all learners need. Many of the same instructional procedures that are appropriate for teaching language arts to all students are just as appropriate for teaching special students. Specific variations of some validated methods make them more effective for teaching special students.

A synthesis of research associated with teaching students with learning and language problems is reported in several publications. At the conclusion of Chapter 1, you will find a listing of selected references containing the mixture of research findings and good practice that provide the basis for appropriate teaching practices. We have used the implications of this research either to document the efficacy or to outline the development of our own CORRECTION strategies throughout this book. We encourage you to refer to these resources for clarification and expanded explanations. The discussion that follows represents an overview of several of the recommended general practices for teaching listening, speaking, reading, and writing skills.

Teach Diagnostically

A particularly important practice for teaching special learners is diagnostic teaching. Beginning with an initial diagnosis to identify specific skill deficits, diagnostic teaching includes targeted instruction for those skill needs and then regular monitoring of skill progress. Monitoring is necessary to determine the appropriateness of methodology, to measure skill gains and needs, and to identify possible instructional modifications.

Special learners need efficient teaching that addresses their individual language skill needs and is tailored to their special learning profiles. They need to be taught precisely what they do not know, using actual classroom materials. Initial assessment of skills should also be curriculum based.

Depending upon the types of skills being monitored, measurement of the effectiveness of instruction might involve calculating the rate of accuracy in answering questions about listening experiences, analyzing speech production trials, charting mispronunciations during reading, or comparing written language samples. Regardless of the exact task and product, some type of charting or graphing of performance across several lessons is required for a record of growth. When performance is not consistently positive, then it is necessary to modify instructional procedures.

Build Language Skills upon Listening Skills

Listening skills are the cornerstone of the language arts. Although the language arts are basically sequential in nature, progressing from listening to speaking and then to reading and writing, it is typically through listening experiences that the other skills are built.

Patterns of speech are learned through early listening experiences. In addition to the language acquired through reading, one's speaking vocabulary is primarily derived from words and concepts understood through listening. It is generally acknowledged that frequent experiences listening to someone read aloud can lead to improved reading performance. Listening, speaking, and reading skills are all utilized in the writing process; however, listening activities are an important part of the planning phase of writing and also provide a logical vehicle for revising written expression. When listening skills are impaired, students are unduly handicapped in all the language arts, requiring adaptations in instructional procedures to allow for the gap or difference in receptive or expressive language processing.

Teach the Language Arts as an Integrated Process

Language is the common denominator of listening, speaking, reading, and writing. By integrating instruction in all the language arts, skills are mutually reinforced and extended. Such coordinated teaching also provides a multisensory approach. When, for example, students are first taught the meaning of a new word in the context of a listening activity, they can also be guided to read the word in a similar or different context, use the word orally or in an elaborated written context, or perhaps use the word in a broader sense, as in a graphic organizer or verbal matrix.

Such integrated experiences help students remember and understand concepts and language patterns as well as increase their opportunities to incorporate the language into their own listening, speaking, reading, and writing patterns. The language experience approach (LEA) illustrates an integrated language method. The LEA has students dictate their experiences to a teacher who writes what they say. Student-generated stories are then used to teach listening, speaking, reading, and writing. For special students, integrated language may be especially meaningful when used along with enjoyable listening and reading experiences.

Build Experiences for Language Development

Students understand and interpret language according to their own experiential backgrounds. Typically, the richer and more varied the experience of the learner, the more meaningful the understanding and language production that will result. For a number of reasons, many special students have had limited experiences participating in a variety of language activities; many also lack the types of experiences that contribute to a general fund of knowledge and language facility. Therefore, teachers must supply numerous concrete experiences to enhance understanding and use of language. Pictures, video and audio materials, and additional oral and written examples also supplement experiences. To promote understanding and use of language, it is necessary to review, extend, or develop concepts and their language labels prior to each lesson. The review may also include prerequisite skills, since some special students tend to forget how and when to apply tentatively mastered skills.

Apply Principles of Behaviorism

Of the practices cited most often as successfully improving the achievement of special students, many incorporate the principles of behaviorism. Based on the premise that rewarded behavior is likely to recur, when designing a plan for teaching language arts skills, two factors should be considered: 1) defining the language behavior to be changed or improved through observation and diagnosis and 2) planning a program to systematically reinforce desired responses.

The first factor is a part of diagnostic teaching but must also include the setting of realistic instructional goals. Lessons must be structured to provide small, manageable steps that will lead to the accomplishment of a designated goal. Systematic reinforcement is somewhat more complicated. You must first determine what constitutes reward and punishment for a specific student. This sometimes becomes apparent by analyzing the instructional conditions that produce desired responses. This procedure is also important for identifying an appropriate stimulus/response format for specific students.

Teach to Learning Style

One strategy that might accelerate academic learning is teaching to individual learning styles, that set of instructional conditions that facilitate a specific student's academic progress. These conditions include the preferred learning modality but add such features as light, sound, time, temperature, grouping, and degree of structure. Preferred stimulus/response format, of which modality is a part, is a key element of a student's learning style. The impact of format is often seen in students whose performance, regardless of knowledge level, varies according to whether the format is oral or written, multiple choice, or fill-in-the-blank.

To illustrate format options, consider reading lessons. The instructional content might include pictures, sentences, paragraphs, stories, poems, listening experiences, or a variety of book, chalkboard, or written stimuli. The responses required of the student may range from selecting a picture or spoken word to saying or writing a letter, word, or paragraph. The type of stimulus you present and response you require determines to a great extent the student's ability to understand and demonstrate knowledge. By nature, the language arts offer a variety of stimulus/response formats that should be explored and manipulated to increase learning rate and performance. Throughout this text, we repeat the need to vary the stimulus/response format according to the student's learning style.

Ask Appropriate Questions

The questions teachers ask determine in part the level of thinking and the degree of understanding that occur. Teachers who routinely ask literal questions are likely to encourage students to think and use language on a literal basis. To become proficient listeners, speakers, readers, and writers, students must also be directed to seek answers to how and why questions and then taught how to respond to them. Appropriate questions stimulate understanding and facilitate problem solving and thinking.

Equally as important as the questions teachers ask are the teachers' responses to students' answers and questions. Teachers who invite and discuss multiple answers and their logical defense increase the quantity and quality of students' responses. Teaching students to formulate their own questions and answers not only increases their understanding of language but also builds vital self-monitoring skills. Teacher behaviors such as using wait time, acknowledging, and restatements are also helpful to students.

Teach Language Arts as a Thinking Process

Closely related to effective questioning is teaching the language arts as a thinking process. Demonstrating and modeling the thought processes are important components of direct instruction in the thinking skills involved in language usage. Guiding students to "think about thinking" and encouraging them to think aloud to reveal their mental manipulations are also key procedures. Students soon become accustomed to thinking aloud and also share their thinking techniques with their peers when they are regularly asked "How did you know that this answer was incorrect?" or instructed to "Prove it out loud" or "Tell us as you think your answer." Such teacher-guided efforts help students develop metacognitive behaviors. The skillful use of language, or languaging, involves more than a single skill, idea, or cognitive process. For many students, combining instruction in language skills with thinking strategies makes retention and transfer of knowledge easier to accomplish.

Use Mapping and Webbing Strategies

Semantic maps, concept maps and webs, word webs, and clustering of vocabulary assist students to understand levels and categories of meaning and to organize their thoughts. The graphic display of the semantic features of language appears to aid students not only to connect the concepts themselves but also to relate them to a specific topic or organizational scheme. Whether formatted as cartoon balloons, tree branches, or concentric circles, the basic premise is the same: Central or major concepts are surrounded by their subordinate concepts in much the same manner as sentences are traditionally diagrammed.

When key words and phrases are categorized and illustrated during the introductory portions of a lesson, students are provided a meaning-based structure for connecting, understanding, and focusing on concepts as they occur in the lesson. As a follow-up listening, reading, or writing experience, students can increase the categorized concepts for clarification or as proof of what has been learned. Using a phased approach, the teacher might begin by supplying several important concepts and then gradually reduce the number of cues until the students can fill in the map based upon what they have learned.

It has been suggested that the visual array of concepts may provide special students with an important learning crutch to facilitate their mastery and memory of the interrelationships of concepts. Mapping is also an aid to language composition. When students are guided to construct maps or webs prior to developing oral or written compositions, these aids function much like outlines; they assist the students to organize and clarify their ideas and then to elaborate on those thoughts. As the compositions evolve, the maps serve as guidelines to help students self-monitor their expression.

Teach Self-Monitoring

In order to become independent learners, students must eventually assume the responsibility for their own language processing. This process entails self-monitoring their understanding of words and ideas. Metacognition is activated as students monitor their learning and self-correct during reading and writing, in particular, and speaking and listening to a lesser degree. As an aid to developing self-monitoring skills and habits, students should be encouraged to verify meanings through the context of what they hear, say, read, or write and to regularly ask themselves questions such as: Did she really say . . .? Do I know that word? Is that what I meant to say? What will happen next? Do I need to reread? Is that sentence complete? Does that make sense?

Before, during, or after an activity, the use of checklists, listening guides, interview guidelines, and graphic organizers assists students to monitor what they hear, say, read, or write. Graphic organizers such as maps and webs help students to monitor their development of oral reports and written compositions. And checklists are valuable tools in determining the need to reread passage parts and in guiding the editing of written work.

Encourage Cooperative Learning

Students as teachers is not a new idea, but it has only been validated as a teaching and learning strategy in recent years. Results from a number of cooperative learning studies verify that students can learn effectively from each other. Since the language arts are the communication skills, cooperative learning groups of two, three, or five students provide a natural environment in which to learn and reinforce language.

It is important to first train the students to use the group format, clarify the nature of each student's role and the sequence of instruction, and then carefully monitor the interaction of each group. Students should model the teacher's effective questioning and responding for their group interactions. Although pairing and grouping students to apply oral and written language is frequently suggested in this book, the teacher must carefully select partners and then guide and monitor their interactions to insure that the format promotes successful experiences.

Use Appropriate Literature and Language Models

A major goal of instruction in language arts is the development of an appreciation of language and good literature. Some materials and activities are better than others for illustrating models of oral and written language. Although the exact model should be selected according to the purpose of the lesson, instruction should also present good, appropriate, and various language formats. When teaching a specific concept or skill, the format options might include a variety of different types of speech, text structures, and writing styles. It is possible to combine purposes so that, for example, while a student is learning to enjoy poetry, he or she is also learning concepts that compliment the current topic of a social studies lesson.

Many skills can also be learned or applied in the context of award-winning literature. Since special students often experience difficulty catching up and then keeping up in most curricular areas, this practice represents an efficient use of teacher and student time and effort. Too frequently, students with special needs are not exposed to interesting and award-winning literature. For each lesson, first consider the language arts skills that a student needs, and then choose the material accordingly. Most school librarians are excellent contacts for recommending good sources. Special sections in *The Horn Book* and *Language Arts* also provide monthly suggestions about good literature for students.

Teach for Mastery

Mastery teaching is an important part of of improving the skills of special students. Since language skills are required for progress in school, teaching for mastery is essential. Many special learners do not easily retain mastery of a skill unless it is frequently reviewed and applied. Such students require systematic instruction over time, periodic reviews, and application of a skill in many and varied language situations. This also involves diagnostic teaching, constant monitoring of skill acquisition, and transfer and reinforcement from one language art to another.

SUMMARY

These thirteen instructional practices are incorporated into the corrective techniques recommended in this book. Perhaps the two most important practices are diagnostic teaching and integration of specific skills into the total language process. The best features of these teaching practices for language learning provide the framework for the CORRECTION strategies in Chapters 4 through 15.

SELECTED REFERENCES

Algozzine, B., & Maheady, L. (Guest Eds.). (1986). In search of excellence: Instruction that works in special education classrooms [Special issue]. *Exceptional Children, 52* (6), 481–608.

Anderson, P. (Ed.). (1983). *Integrating reading, writing, and thinking*. Urbana, IL: National Council of Teachers of English.

Anderson, P. S., & Lapp, D. (1988). *Language skills in elementary education*. New York: Macmillan.

Bromley, K. D. (1988). *Language arts: Exploring connections*. Boston: Allyn and Bacon.

Gaskins, I. W. (Guest Ed.). (1988). Teaching poor readers: What works [Special Issue]. *The Reading Teacher, 41* (8), 748–972.

Gelzheiser, L. M., & Shepherd, M. J. (Guest Eds.). (1986). Competence and instruction: Contributions from cognitive psychology [Special issue]. *Exceptional Children, 53* (2), 97–192.

Graham, S., & Harris, K. R. (Guest Eds.) (1988). Research and instruction in written language [Special issue]. *Exceptional Children, 54* (6), 491–584.

Harris, A. J., & Sipay, E. R. (1985). *How to increase reading ability: A guide to developmental and remedial methods* (8th ed.). White Plains, NY: Longman.

Hillocks, G., Jr. (1987). Synthesis of research on teaching writing. *Educational Leadership*, 44 (8), 71–82.

Hutson, B. A. (Ed.) (1985). *Advances in reading/language research* (Vol. 3). Greenwich, CT: JAI Press.

Just, M. A., & Carpenter, P. A. (1987). *The psychology of reading and language comprehension*. Boston: Allyn and Bacon.

Meyen, E. L., Vergason, G. A., & Whelan, R. J. (Eds.) (1983). *Promising practices for exceptional children: Curriculum implications*. Denver: Love.

Monson, D. L., Taylor, B. M., & Dykstra, R. (1988). *Language arts: Teaching and learning effective use of language*. Glenview, IL: Scott, Foresman.

Myers, M., & Gray, J. (Eds.) (1983). *Theory and practice in the teaching of comprehension: Processing, distancing, and modeling*. Urbana, IL: National Council of Teachers of English.

Squires, D. A., Huitt, W. G., & Segars, J. K. (1984). *Effective schools and classrooms: A research-based perspective*. Alexandria, VA: Association for Supervision and Curriculum Development.

Wang, M. C., Reynolds, M. C., & Walberg, H. J. (Eds.). (1987). *Handbook of special education: Research and practice* (Vol. 1–2). New York: Pergamon Press.

CUMULATIVE-DEFICIT STUDENTS

DETECTION These students may:

- Demonstrate a pattern of steadily decreasing performance in all subjects
- Have difficulty reading and writing but not speaking and listening
- Pronounce, understand, and spell review words but not new ones
- Evidence language-skill and/or concept gaps

Description. Students with this problem are often described by teachers as the ones who "got behind and can't catch up." They simply did not master the prerequisite skills before the language arts curriculum moved on ahead of them. These problems are most obvious in their reading and writing.

Causation. Cumulative deficits occur when students do not master key language skills at the intended point in the curriculum; then, lacking prerequisite skills, the deficits are compounded as new skills are introduced and levels of difficulty increased. Frequent or lengthy absences, a change in schools, and fragmented instruction caused by teacher error or absences tend to interrupt program and skill continuity. Additional problems such as narrow vocabularies, limited experiences, or lack of reinforcement at home further contribute to the problem. Some students become so overwhelmed that they simply quit trying.

Implications. A cumulative deficit in language arts skills eventually interferes with performance in all subject areas. Classwork is often incomplete or incorrect because it is too difficult and/or the strategies are not mastered. As these students advance in school, demands for independent classwork increase while their overall academic performances decrease.

CORRECTIVE PRINCIPLES Use these guidelines to plan and modify instruction.

1. Directly teach the specific skills that impede progress.
2. Temporarily slow instructional pace to permit reteaching of skills.
3. Review and reteach prerequisite skills and concepts before each lesson.
4. Teach concepts and mechanics with focused listening activities.
5. Provide a tutor for supplementary instruction in appropriate prerequisites.
6. Use cooperative learning groups for language assignments.

CULTURALLY/LANGUAGE-DIFFERENT STUDENTS

DETECTION These students may:

- Perform most language arts tasks below capacity level
- Display a restricted vocabulary
- Use incorrect grammar and have difficulty with complex sentences
- Frequently mispronounce, rearrange, or substitute words
- Comprehend surface meanings only

Description. Students whose primary language and/or culture differs from that of the predominant culture of the schools may display language arts difficulties that range from mild to severe. Their specific problems tend to resemble many of those exhibited by language-disabled students. Their language performance is often riddled with errors in pronunciation, syntax, and vocabulary. Silent reading comprehension may be less difficult for them than oral reading comprehension or comprehension of speech.

Causation. Many of these students think in their primary language and then translate into English. This means that some of the idiosyncracies of the first language often creep into their translations, producing errors consistent with the student's dialect or language. The translation process also slows language processing. Idiomatic and figurative language are often translated literally. Some teachers expect less achievement from these students and thus cause them to achieve less.

Implications. The language differences often complicate the learner's task in all the language arts as well as in other subjects. The use of pictures and other visual cues to explain and translate concepts is helpful in all subjects. The cultural differences that accompany language differences often mean experiential backgrounds that differ from those of the school majority. Thus, common experiences must be established or explained prior to each lesson. The focus of instruction should be on comprehension and communication, not on exact pronunciation or grammatical structure.

CORRECTIVE PRINCIPLES Use these guidelines to plan and modify instruction.

1. Build concrete and vicarious experiences prior to each lesson.
2. Use pictures and other visual cues to explain and translate concepts.
3. Give students the written script of oral directions and lessons.
4. Encourage oral communication through structured discussions, giving positive corrective feedback for vocabulary and grammatical regularities.
5. Use choral speaking and reading activities to improve oral fluency.
6. Use a language experience approach to bridge the gap between students' oral language, reading, and writing and to explain syntactical differences.

SLOW-LEARNING STUDENTS

DETECTION These students may:

- Develop language skills at a slower rate than most age peers
- Require more practice and repetition than most age peers
- Have narrow vocabularies
- Take longer to perform reading and writing tasks than age peers
- Make steady but slow progress with individualized instruction

Description. These students are often described as those who "always lag behind the rest of the class." Although the skill sequence of the regular language arts curriculum is appropriate for these students, they typically take longer to master each task. A slightly slower pace and additional instruction and reinforcement are required for them to master the important language skills.

Causation. These students need not experience difficulties if the pace of the language arts curriculum is adjusted to their slower rate of learning. However, the typical problems occur when the pace of the curriculum leaves them behind. Facing new and more difficult language tasks before mastering the prerequisite skills, their skill deficits begin to accumulate. Much like the students described as exhibiting cumulative deficits, factors such as narrow vocabularies, limited experiential backgrounds, and limited reinforcement or practice at home further contribute to the problem.

Implications. Although these students may not advance a full achievement level in all the language arts each school year, many can master the most basic of skills. Typically, their slow learning rate is not confined to the language arts but is reflected in their overall academic performance. They may require not only supplementary instruction but also special assistance as they attempt independent tasks.

CORRECTIVE PRINCIPLES Use these guidelines to plan and modify instruction.

1. Slow the pace of instruction to match the student's learning rate.
2. Provide extended readiness and practice activities for each lesson.
3. Review and reteach prerequisite skills before each lesson.
4. Provide ample talking and listening activities to expand language skills.
5. Directly teach word meanings with word-analysis and spelling skills.
6. Shorten assignments to manageable units.
7. Emphasize real-life language arts skills.

TEACHER-DISABLED STUDENTS

DETECTION These students may:

- Evidence gaps in language arts skills
- Apply language arts skills inappropriately
- Either try very hard or not at all
- Have difficulty understanding and/or expressing language
- Perform at a slow rate

Description. Teacher-disabled students are those who have been taught incorrectly or ineffectively. The language performances of these students often fall at one of two extremes: either the student obviously exerts a tremendous amount of effort or he or she appears to have given up in defeat. Many of these students appear to know only one strategy for each task; for example, some concentrate on punctuation at the expense of expressing ideas.

Causation. The causes of students' becoming teacher disabled are varied and are often suspected after the fact. The prime offenders are the nonteachers, who put the textbooks and workbooks with the children and assume learning will just happen; those who teach the textbook and not the students, insisting that the entire class advance together according to the teacher's agenda; or those who emphasize the mechanics and not the content of language. Other contributors include frequent teacher absences, inadequate planning, and changes in textbook series, as well as teachers being too rigid and teacher-student personality conflicts that result in aversive learning experiences. Some teachers overemphasize one skill at the expense of others, producing students who persist in using only the one strategy, while other teachers actually teach specific students that they are hopeless. Although these are initially teacher problems, not student problems, they eventually result in the students' exhibiting academic problems.

Implications. Students who, without success, conscientiously follow the instructions of their teachers soon lose faith in themselves and in their education. Without intervention, they are destined to experience difficulty in all the language arts as well as in subjects across the academic curriculum. A product of ineffective strategies, the slow performance rates of many of these students may be reflected in incomplete assignments in all subjects.

CORRECTIVE PRINCIPLES Use these guidelines to plan and modify instruction.

1. Identify and fill language-skill gaps.
2. Review and reteach prerequisite skills before each lesson.
3. Use listening and speaking activities to teach reading and writing skills.
4. Stress the content of language, rather than the mechanics.
5. Carefully structure language arts experiences to insure students' success.

UNDERACHIEVING STUDENTS

DETECTION These students may:

- Exhibit language arts skills below the level teachers expect
- Perform inconsistently and be distractible
- Appear to dislike and avoid the rigors of academic work
- Perform much better when topics are of high interest
- Often comprehend surface meanings only

Description.   Underachievers usually exhibit similar performances across school subjects. They are the students who do not appear to exert much effort to perform and who most often seem disinterested. These students occasionally perform voluntarily when a topic appeals to them and even show sudden bursts of skill gains but soon lose their enthusiasm. Many of these students seem to be easily distracted in the classroom.

Causation.   The causes of underachievement are many and varied. Lack of motivation is often the primary factor. This may result from sociocultural values in conflict with those of the school, lack of reinforcement for academic achievement, negative role models, or inability to see the relevance of language arts to personal goals in particular and academic achievement in general. Teacher pressure may only compound the problem. Language differences, little exposure to positive academic experiences, limited experiential background, and inadequate educational training can also contribute to underachievement. Students who are easily distracted or too stimulated by a classful of peers are particularly hindered when attempting to concentrate on reading and writing. The possibility of specific learning differences, such as those described in the next chapter, should also be considered.

Implications.   Students who achieve significantly below their capacity do so at the cost of not developing the skills prerequisite to future progress in language arts and in most other subjects. They often appear to exert little effort, and their verbal expression and understanding may be sparse. Many teachers tend to be impatient and negative in their interactions with these students. Some teachers try to make underachievers perform, thereby producing a pronounced dislike for academic work. An important part of correction is identifying the cause(s) of a student's underachievement.

CORRECTIVE PRINCIPLES Use these guidelines to plan and modify instruction.

1. Identify the cause of underachievement and then teach accordingly.
2. Determine students' interests and then plan appropriate activities.
3. Focus on activities that emphasize the usefulness of the language arts.
4. Clearly state the purposes of each language arts activity.
5. Personalize the language arts activities for relevance and meaning.

CROSS-CATEGORICAL HANDICAPPED STUDENTS

DETECTION Properly identified students may:

- Have difficulty attending or comprehending while listening
- Have problems with oral expression
- Demonstrate reading skills below the level of age peers
- Exhibit particular difficulty in written expression
- Evidence some of the specific problems cited by the exceptional categories on the pages that follow

Description. To be classified as handicapped, students must be appropriately evaluated and meet their state's criteria for eligibility for special education services. Instead of providing special education services according to the exact category of students' exceptionalities, some school systems group students in a generic or cross-categorical fashion according to the severity of the handicap. Thus, students whose disability is of a mild to moderate degree and who evidence many of the learning characteristics of several categories of exceptionalities are placed in cross-categorical settings for mild/moderately handicapped. In addition to any special education these students receive, many of them receive a large portion, and sometimes all, of their instruction in a regular education classroom. In the areas of listening and speaking, many of these students perform below the level of their age peers. A large percentage of them experience a number of problems mastering reading skills, and an even greater proportion find written expression significantly difficult. These students also exhibit some of the patterns of language arts performance more typical of one or more categorical exceptionalities.

Causation. These students qualify for special education services on the basis of their unique learning needs for adjusted instruction and curricula. These same specific needs often interfere with the orderly acquisition of the skills required for effective language usage. Among the characteristics shared by many of these students are short attention span, distractibility, need for success and encouragement, both listening and reading comprehension difficulties, receptive and/or expressive language deficits, narrow vocabularies, patterns of word-recognition and spelling problems, limited experiences, and the need for individualized and specialized instruction in one or more of the language arts. Some of these learning characteristics appear to complicate the tasks of the language arts curriculum, while others directly interfere with achievement.

Implications. Although these students share many common needs in mastering the language arts, differences in their learning characteristics produce varied profiles of performance. Yet most of their skill patterns indicate both general and specific problems in one or more of the language arts. The difficulties they experience in mastering listening, speaking, reading, and writing tasks most often result in difficulties across the academic curricula. Refer to the treatments of the needs of related exceptional categories for specific examples of the interactions of learning characteristics and language arts performances.

CORRECTIVE PRINCIPLES

Much of the impetus for cross-categorical or generic groupings grew out of the realization that numerous common principles of corrective instruction applied to mild/moderately handicapped students in several exceptional categories. Many of these principles are equally appropriate for teaching the language arts to nonhandicapped students. They reflect the concerns of structuring the learning environment, building appropriate experiences and attitudes, and adjusting the content and style of instruction to the learners' needs. In addition to the teaching practices recommended in Chapter 1, use these general principles as guidelines to plan and modify instruction in the language arts for mildly and moderately handicapped students.

1. Build and recall experiences to prepare students for each learning task and to broaden language knowledge.
2. Determine learning strengths and then vary stimulus/response patterns according to students' needs.
3. Present short and varied instructional tasks planned to insure student success.
4. Keep distractions to a minimum in the classroom.
5. Systematically reinforce appropriate performance.
6. Consider students' interests as well as level of difficulty when selecting instructional materials.
7. Include review material or tasks as the major portion of each language arts activity, providing periodic review and reinforcement activities.
8. Use listening activities to build speaking skills.
9. Build reading skills upon listening and speaking skills.
10. Use listening, speaking, and reading skills to build writing skills.
11. Emphasize the usefulness and relevance of the language arts and clearly state the purpose for presenting each task.
12. Routinely collaborate with appropriate specialists to design and modify each student's language arts program.

BEHAVIOR-DISORDERED STUDENTS

DETECTION Properly identified students may:

- Exhibit inappropriate behaviors that interfere with academic ⟍ progress
- Have problems or be reluctant to communicate orally and/or in writing
- Seem capable of achieving at a higher level
- Have difficulty attending or comprehending while listening
- Be slow to begin or complete tasks or perform quickly and carelessly
- Become agitated when difficult assignments are encountered

Description. The nature of the language arts difficulty is dependent in part upon the particular manifestation of the behavioral difficulty. When students' performance is adversely affected, it is often reflected in unsatisfactory rates, inaccuracy, poor group interaction, off-task behavior, and avoidance of interpersonal interactions and escalation of negative behavior when the tasks become difficult.

Causation. The language problems experienced by these students are often a logical outgrowth of their behaviors. Distractibility interferes with on-task behavior. Insecurity in unstructured or changed learning situations impedes performance. Overcautiousness and distrust create careful but slow workers, while impulsivity results in fast but careless workers. Low frustration tolerance causes defeat when facing difficult tasks. Disruptive behaviors interfere with the performance of self and others. Group activities overstimulate some students, while intimidating others. Depressed language functioning is symptomatic of some types of behavior disorders.

Implications. Behavior-disordered students do not necessarily exhibit difficulties in language arts. In fact, some become proficient readers and writers who use these skills as an escape. However, many satisfactorily perform independent assignments but not interactive assignments. The major threat to academic performance is the interruption in sequenced skill mastery, which may eventually result in a cumulative language deficit.

CORRECTIVE PRINCIPLES Use these guidelines to plan and modify instruction.

1. Contract with students for specific skills and then chart progress.
2. Plan highly structured programs, using a consistent stimulus/response format, routine, and positive reinforcement.
3. Accommodate students' attention spans and their frustration-tolerance levels.
4. Plan lessons that can be accomplished with the teacher or alone; gradually phase in interactive activities.
5. Select bibliotherapeutic themes for lesson content.
6. Directly teach independent study skills along with the language arts.

HEARING-IMPAIRED STUDENTS

DETECTION Properly identified students may:

- Evidence difficulty in all the language arts
- Exhibit specific problems in speaking, reading, and/or spelling
- Master language skills slowly
- Have a very limited vocabulary
- Have difficulty producing and comprehending complex sentences

Description. Students who are hearing impaired often evidence many of the sam
difficulties as those with general language disorders and some of the prob
lems of those with speech disorders. Their command of language is often
inversely proportional to the degree of hearing loss. Subtle phonetic differences may escape their attention, as may word meanings and comple
sentences. They tend to require extensive instruction and practice to master language arts skills.

Causation. Because this disability directly interferes with mastery of listening
skills, these students miss many of the opportunities for language growth
and for reinforcement of the concepts and skills involved in speaking,
reading, and writing. They tend to struggle with pronunciation, meaning,
and manipulation of words and ideas. They must strain to hear, draw from
an often sparse vocabulary to express ideas, monitor their speech, struggle
with subtle meanings, and reauditorize the words needed to express their
ideas. Many hesitate to interact verbally, thereby further limiting improvement and demonstration of language achievement. They tend to tire
quickly and must have shortened lessons, but they require extended time
to master language tasks.

Implications. Like students with language disorders, these students tend to experience particular difficulty in learning and improving language skills.
They often miss much of the incidental learning available to their hearing
peers. Their narrow vocabularies and difficulties understanding subtle
meanings interfere with progress in language arts and in all academic
areas. Many must use sight and touch as a compensatory learning
technique.

CORRECTIVE PRINCIPLES Use these guidelines to plan and modify instruction.

1. Integrate the language arts and speech/language development
   programs.
2. Seat students where they can best see and hear.
3. Teach the use of sight and touch as a compensatory learning technique.
4. Present visual cues for each task, alternating auditory and visual
   assignments.
5. Carefully build the experiential framework before each lesson.
6. Extend the readiness and practice activities for each lesson.
7. Offer extensive training in word and sentence meanings.

LANGUAGE-DISABLED STUDENTS

DETECTION Properly identified students may:

- Evidence a specific language comprehension difficulty
- Have difficulty conversing or explaining answers
- Pronounce words but often do not know their meanings
- Have a limited or inappropriate vocabulary
- Use incorrect grammar

Description. Understanding the meanings of single words, phrases, and whole passages can be particularly difficult for language-disabled students. Although they may correctly pronounce words, they may miss the meanings of passages or words. They may read aloud skillfully but understand little of what they pronounce. Some have difficulty understanding listening activities and conversation; others appear to search for the words to say or write.

Causation. The language problems of these students are generally ones of meaning. Difficulties receiving and interpreting language interfere with understanding the words and ideas of listening activities, oral directions, conversation, and reading passages. Because of their inability to manipulate words and ideas, they are also denied much of the incidental learning that occurs from various language interactions. Difficulties expressing thoughts, whether verbally or in writing, may interfere with their expressive performance and with their demonstrating what they do know and understand.

Implications. The language emphasis of a language arts programs creates particular difficulties for these students. Their problems often interfere with performance in all academic tasks that involve language. Some students may actually understand speech and text but are unable to formulate the words to express their knowledge. Thus, when asked to select correct answers, as in a multiple-choice activity, they can demonstrate their understanding, but when asked to express their knowledge in short-answer or essay form, they cannot. Often classroom directions and oral explanations are not fully understood, leading to misinterpretations that further compound the problems.

CORRECTIVE PRINCIPLES Use these guidelines to plan and modify instruction.

1. Integrate the language arts and language development programs.
2. Build a background of concrete experiences for each lesson.
3. With each concept, teach both receptive and expressive tasks.
4. Provide intensive instruction in word, sentence, and passage meanings.
5. Supplement instruction with visual aids.
6. Evaluate performance by having students select the correct answer.
7. Provide positive corrective feedback for language skills.

LEARNING-DISABLED STUDENTS

DETECTION Properly identified students may:

- Evidence inconsistent and uneven performance of language arts tasks
- Demonstrate listening and speaking skills superior to reading and writing skills
- Exhibit language-skill gaps
- Be easily distracted from academic tasks
- Appear capable of performing at a higher achievement level

Description. Many learning-disabled students exhibit problems in language arts, often characterized by a disparity between actual and potential achievement levels. The exact manifestation of their difficulties, however, varies widely. Many are easily distracted from academic tasks. Some find listening and speaking frustrating; many experience specific problems reading; most exhibit some degree of writing difficulty. The most extreme cases exhibit deficits in all areas of the language arts.

Causation. Primarily a heterogeneous group, learning-disabled students typically exhibit a disparity between achievement and capacity levels or across subject areas. Many of their learning characteristics compound their language difficulties: hyperactivity, distractibility, and short attention spans interrupt on-task behaviors; fluctuating performances frustrate both students and teachers; and apparent processing difficulties further confuse students. Adjusting the stimulus/response requirements of classroom tasks to their needs tends to increase their performance as does multisensory instruction.

Implications. The language problems of the learning disabled are varied and often complex. The same inconsistencies evident in their performance of these tasks appear across curricular areas. And many of the instructional strategies that increase language progress also improve performance in other subject areas.

CORRECTIVE PRINCIPLES Use these guidelines to plan and modify instruction.

1. Adjust stimulus/response patterns, permitting the interchange of language skills as needed.
2. Teach students strategies to compensate for specific learning weaknesses.
3. Build study and independent learning skills.
4. Use visual and auditory prompts to teach each lesson.
5. Prepare brief activities and vary the types of activities.
6. Provide a nondistracting learning environment.
7. Use each of the language arts to reinforce the others.

MENTALLY RETARDED STUDENTS

DETECTION Properly identified students may:

- Develop language skills at a much slower rate than age peers
- Exhibit a limited vocabulary
- Need concrete objects and experiences to master language concepts
- Be unable to remember words or concepts without numerous repetitions
- Have difficulty comprehending complex language

Description. The limited intellectual capacity of mentally retarded students similarly limits their language skills. Their rate of progress is noticeably slow. They require extended time and instruction to master language tasks, although the sequence of skill mastery is that of the regular curriculum. While they may master the rudiments of such mechanical tasks as spelling and phonics, they learn writing and comprehension skills very slowly and laboriously.

Causation. Most of the academic problems experienced by these students are a reflection of their limited language and thinking skills. Due to the narrow language skills, these students often have difficulty understanding and expressing the meanings of words and ideas. The higher levels of cognitive processing required for interpretive and critical comprehension and writing are particularly difficult. These students tend to overlook subtle meanings and miss opportunities for peripheral and incidental learning.

Implications. Because of their slow rate of learning, these students should not be expected to attempt the pace of the regular language arts curriculum. This slow progress is not confined to language arts but permeates their academic performance. Mentally retarded students particularly need direct instruction to recognize, understand, and use terms essential to following oral and written directions, social functioning, and survival outside the classroom.

CORRECTIVE PRINCIPLES Use these guidelines to plan and modify instruction.

1. Focus on the language arts skills needed for real-life functioning.
2. Use concrete objects and experiences to teach language concepts.
3. Teach each concept very slowly, reviewing frequently.
4. Often repeat instruction and practice for each task.
5. Extend the readiness activities for each language lesson, building prerequisite skills and concepts.
6. Use each of the language arts to reinforce the others.
7. Carefully divide sentences by thought units to facilitate both oral and written comprehension.

PHYSICALLY/MEDICALLY HANDICAPPED STUDENTS

DETECTION Properly identified students may:

- Read and write at a slow rate
- Evidence a narrow vocabulary
- Demonstrate inconsistent performances across language areas
- Have difficulty with comprehension, interpretation, or written expression
- Exhibit language-skill gaps

Description. Physically/medically handicapped students have physical or health problems that so limit their classroom performance that they are eligible for special education services. When the skills of language arts are adversely affected, it is often in the areas of word and text meanings, performance rate, and specific gaps across or in the sequence of the language arts skills.

Causation. Skill gaps may result from frequent absences from school because of physical and medical complications. The physical adjustments some students must make to accomplish reading and writing tasks often require such strain and effort that the students perform slowly and tire quickly. Physical and health limitations similarly limit the range of available experiences; this lack of experience may be reflected in shallow comprehension and narrow receptive and expressive vocabularies. School performances often fluctuate in direct relation to the condition of the student's health.

Implications. The nature of the physical or medical handicap determines the degree, if any, of interference with performance. Students who are mobile, attend school regularly, and feel well most of the time do not necessarily experience academic difficulty resulting from the handicap. Alterations in the classroom environment— including changes in the physical structure of the classroom itself, the stimulus/response patterns, and the use of mechanical devices— can compensate for many physical limitations and accommodate students' needs in the language arts. However, slow performance, skill gaps, and the need for additional experiences and vocabulary expansion may slow progress in reading and written expression, as well as in other subject areas.

CORRECTIVE PRINCIPLES Use these guidelines to plan and modify instruction.

1. Adjust the physical environment to accommodate students' needs.
2. Broaden the experiential repertoire and extend preparation for each lesson.
3. Vary the stimulus/response pattern according to students' needs.
4. To avoid fatigue, rely heavily on oral activities and present short and varied reading and writing tasks.
5. Conduct much of the instruction as listening and speaking exercises.
6. Provide intensive instruction and experiences to broaden vocabularies.
7. Teach students to independently adjust for physical and learning needs.

SPEECH-DISORDERED STUDENTS

DETECTION Properly identified students may:

- Have difficulty discriminating certain sounds
- Be reluctant to speak or read aloud before others
- Be unable to speak or read aloud fluently or with appropriate voice
- Comprehend better when reading silently than when reading orally
- Express thoughts better through writing than speaking

Description. Speech disorders are of three types: articulation, fluency, and voice. Each generally distorts the student's oral language. Students may appear reluctant to read, discuss, or answer aloud. For some, certain sounds are particularly difficult to discriminate and/or produce. Silent comprehension is often easier for these students, as they are freed from the task of pronunciation and may attend to meaning.

Causation. The particular type of speech disorder generally determines the nature and degree of interference with oral reading and answering. Problems of articulation result in consistent mispronunciations of specific sounds and words. Fluency difficulties cause the repetition or prolonging of certain sounds. Voice disorders result in inappropriate pitch, intensity, or quality of voice and cause the voice to tire easily. The speech effort and distortions often interfere with oral communication.

Implications. Speech disorders need not interfere with progress in the language arts. Silent or written work is seldom affected, despite difficulties communicating orally. Some of these students must focus great effort and concentration on production of sounds. Although some dysfluencies disappear during oral reading or singing, they are most evident in conversation or when orally answering questions. The most obvious interference with language arts performance is the reluctance of students to voluntarily read, discuss, or answer aloud, thus limiting oral interaction and the display of skills and knowledge. Embarrassed teachers and peers tend to limit the student's opportunities to demonstrate his or her true achievements. Instruction in discriminating and producing troublesome sounds, syllables, or words should be coordinated by the speech pathologist, while a medical specialist must designate appropriate oral activities for students with voice problems.

CORRECTIVE PRINCIPLES Use these guidelines to plan and modify instruction.

1. Integrate the language arts and speech therapy programs.
2. Encourage oral interaction in a supportive environment.
3. Provide corrective feedback in a positive manner.
4. Offer ample opportunities to practice fluent speech.
5. Permit silent reading and written answers as needed.
6. Build language skills through listening, talking, and choral activities.

VISUALLY IMPAIRED STUDENTS

DETECTION Properly identified students may:

- Master reading and writing skills slowly
- Listen and speak much better than they read and write
- Perform at a slow rate
- Hold books and papers at an odd distance and lose their place on the page
- Have difficulty understanding implied meanings

Description. Students who are visually impaired learn language skills in much the same way as their sighted peers but may learn to read and write at a slower pace. To the partially sighted, print may appear distorted and/or blurred. They often must carefully study the page to make sense of it and point to each word to keep their place. Although written responses may be easier for these students to accomplish, they must struggle to proofread and locate their responses. These processes slow the performance rate.

Causation. Denied the range and quantity of visual stimulation and learning of their sighted peers, these students often bring only limited experiences to the reading and writing processes. Although some may even exhibit advanced listening and speaking skills, many require additional concrete experiences, such as auditory and tactile examples, to expand and enrich their concepts and vocabularies. The effort and time required to form and decipher print seem to interfere with reading and writing performance.

Implications. Given sufficient auditory support, visually impaired students can steadily build upon their speaking and listening skills to improve reading and writing. However, their tendency to perform at a slower rate and to take longer to master reading and writing skills interferes with their ability to maintain the pace of the typical language arts curriculum. For the partially sighted, many classroom routines are particularly difficult to achieve; thus, these students may fall behind peers both in language arts progress and demonstrating task mastery. Shortened assignments, oral responses, and keyboarded assignments instead of written ones may facilitate progress and prevent students from tiring from strain. Visually impaired and blind students must learn to use such compensatory techniques as hearing, touch, or even Braille to progress in language arts.

CORRECTIVE PRINCIPLES Use these guidelines to plan and modify instruction.

1. Seat students where they can best see and hear the teacher.
2. Carefully build both real and vicarious experiences for each lesson.
3. Present auditory cues for each visual task.
4. Limit visual strain by using auditory and oral stimulus/response patterns.
5. Provide extensive training in word and concept meanings.
6. Emphasize listening skills in teaching the other language arts skills.

ACADEMICALLY GIFTED STUDENTS

DETECTION Properly identified students may:

- Have a large and expansive vocabulary and use complex sentences and syntax
- Read and write above age peers and/or well below ability level
- Learn faster than age peers but display skill gaps
- Be critical readers and writers and sometimes bored with lesson content
- Perform drill grudgingly, incompletely, or not at all
- Excel in language content but not in details or mechanics

Description. Most academically gifted students read and write well beyond the levels that they have been taught. Many have rich vocabularies and the capacity for a deep understanding of language. However, many perform below their actual capacity level and evidence skill gaps. Special problems of some gifted students include underachievement or undetected talent. Such students may have limited vocabularies or background experiences, specific skill deficits, and may even avoid language tasks. As a group, gifted students tend to perform drill reluctantly. Many make careless errors in spelling and writing.

Causation. Many gifted students prove to themselves that they can perform a task and then lose interest. Their rapid learning rate often results in disdain for boring, meaningless drill. Skill gaps occur because many of their skills are often self-taught. Underachievement may result from conformity with school or sociocultural expectations, inadequate experiential background, or a handicapping condition. Because some gifted students tend to overlook details in written work, their grades in language arts often do not reflect their true abilities.

Implications. Many gifted students can advance rapidly in language arts skills when taught specific strategies and provided opportunities to do so. This enables them to master content in many subjects independently and progress at their own rates and levels, which will help prevent many of the academic problems and classroom behaviors typical of unchallenged students. They need to be freed of the boundaries of the regular curriculum.

CORRECTIVE PRINCIPLES Use these guidelines to plan and modify instruction.

1. Use an individualized approach to teach language arts.
2. Fill in skill gaps as needed.
3. Offer enriched, challenging language experiences.
4. Directly teach study and research skills.
5. Avoid repetitious drill, allowing students to advance as able.
6. Encourage students to evaluate, rewrite, and create text.
7. Teach the skills of debate and then provide opportunities for practice.

REFLECTIONS

1. The four areas of the language arts are so closely related that instruction in one often builds upon or provides instruction in the others. Select a writing lesson from an elementary English textbook; analyze the lesson to determine the prerequisite language skills as well as the listening, speaking, and/or reading skills that can be taught in the same lesson.

2. Each of the 13 teaching practices described in Chapter 1 applies to more than one of the language arts. Develop three of your own examples of the application of one of these practices to teach listening, speaking, reading, and writing.

3. The organization of Part I suggests differences in the language arts needs of students in regular/remedial classes and those who are classified as exceptional. Compare and contrast a problem in each area. Are there distinct differences in the DETECTION behaviors and in the CORRECTIVE PRINCIPLES? Why or why not?

4. Many of the CORRECTIVE PRINCIPLES apply to all students. Justify the selection of the ones presented, adding principles where you deem necessary. Consider how each principle could be used to structure the teaching of each of the areas of language arts: listening, speaking, reading, and writing.

5. Problems in language arts tend to assume different proportions according to the student population and the perceptions of individual teachers. Interview a highly skilled regular education teacher to determine his or her perception of the important DETECTION behaviors and CORRECTIVE PRINCIPLES for each categorized problem; then discuss detection and correction of any frequent problems that are not mentioned in Chapter 2. Follow a similar procedure to interview a veteran special education teacher.

6. Many school systems offer cross-categorical special education services, grouping all mildly handicapped students for instruction. Reread the DETECTION behaviors and the CORRECTIVE PRINCIPLES cited for the exceptional classifications; add your own observations. Then debate the value of categorical and noncategorical special education training in language arts. Consider the advantages and disadvantages of each model to the individual students, to the other students in the class, to the teacher, and to the school system.

7. The CORRECTIVE PRINCIPLES are suggested as guides for selecting and modifying strategies for teaching the language arts. Select a hypothetical special learner; use the CORRECTIVE PRINCIPLES to modify a typical lesson in a language textbook for that learner. Repeat the process for a second special learner. Compare and contrast the two lessons. For the same content, review the lesson script in the teacher's edition of the text. How do your lessons differ from the ones suggested for most students?

8. Special learners often need very focused and carefully planned lessons. Plan one or more integrated language arts lessons for a special learner. Take the content of your lesson from the reading and language textbooks currently in use in the student's school. Use the diagnostic information available from the school, the general teaching practices in Chapter 1, and the CORRECTIVE PRINCIPLES to guide the design of your lessons.

9. Targeted lessons for special learners involve very precise instruction. Implement the integrated language arts lessons you designed for a special

learner. As you teach, note the particular learning characteristics and the skill needs of the student as information for planning future lessons.

10. In addition to the selected references given in Chapter 1, a number of language arts and special education textbooks address the special needs of students with learning or experience problems. Compare and contrast discussions in these sources with the information in Part I:

Gearheart, B. R., Weishahn, M., & Gearheart, C. J. (1988). *The exceptional student in the regular classroom* (4th ed.). Columbus, OH: Charles E. Merrill.

Gloeckler, T. & Simpson, C. (1988). *Exceptional students in regular classrooms: Challenges, services, and methods.* Mountain View, CA: Mayfield.

Henderson, E. H. (1984). *Teaching children to spell English.* Boston: Houghton Mifflin.

Hennings, D. G. (1986). *Communication in action: Teaching the language arts* (3rd ed.). Boston: Houghton Mifflin.

Hoskisson, K., & Tompkins, G. E. (1987). *Language arts: Content and teaching strategies.* Columbus, OH: Charles E. Merrill.

Lewis, R. B., & Doorlag, D. H. (1987). *Teaching special students in the mainstream* (2nd ed.). Columbus, OH: Charles E. Merrill.

McCoy, K., & Prehm, H. J. (1987). *Teaching mainstreamed students: Methods and techniques.* Denver: Love.

Norton, D. E. (1985). *The effective teaching of language arts* (2nd ed.). Columbus, OH: Charles E. Merrill.

Petty, W. T., Petty, D. C., & Becking, M. F. (1985). *Experiences in language art methods* (4th ed.). Boston: Allyn and Bacon.

Schloss, P. J., & Sedlak, R. A. (1986). *Instructional methods for students with learning and behavior problems.* Boston: Allyn and Bacon.

Wallace, G., Cohen, S. B., & Polloway, E. A. (1987). *Language arts: Teaching exceptional students.* Austin, TX: Pro-Ed.

Wallace, G., & Kauffman, J. M. (1986). *Teaching students with learning and behavior problems* (3rd ed.). Columbus, OH: Charles E. Merrill.

PART II

SPECIAL LISTENING NEEDS

Listening, like reading, is a receptive language skill. The listening skills provide the foundation upon which to build the other language arts. A prime channel for classroom learning in all subjects, listening activities generally represent a major portion of instructional methodology. Through listening activities, students build language skills, expand vocabularies, enrich experiences, learn concepts, understand the mechanics for specific tasks, develop readiness skills for particular lessons, appreciate the joys of spoken and written language, and even relax. Listening is a set of learned skills, incidentally acquired by some students but mastered only through direct instruction by many.

Despite the infusion of listening activities throughout academic curricula, when recorded on progress reports, listening skills are often evaluated negatively as classroom conduct with such comments as "does not listen" or "does not pay attention." Briefly cited but seldom explained, listening is not typically accorded its proper place in formal written curricula. For these reasons, listening has been described as the "forgotten" language art or the "skill of assumption."

In Part II, three chapters provide the framework for identifying and providing for instructional needs in listening skills. The skills of attentive listening are approached in Chapter 4, beginning with the attention and recognition of auditory stimuli. Once the sounds are accurately perceived, the listener must interpret and understand at least their surface meanings, which is not an easy task for students who are culturally different or who come to school speaking a dialect that varies from standard English.

Chapter 5, "Auditory Memory," represents the most typical treatment and discussion of listening skills. Four skills are discussed: following directions, remembering general information, recalling in sequence, and critical listening. The first three involve perception and then interpretation. Critical listening requires the listener to judge and evaluate the content of the message, an important academic skill that is even more important in real life.

Chapter 6, "Auditory Appreciation," covers the skills that even the best teachers often overlook. These are the skills that help students become comfortable listening and interacting with people or good literature. The overall purpose of this chapter is to suggest ways for improving listening skills as a learning channel and to highlight the pleasures of listening.

DETECTION OF SPECIAL LISTENING NEEDS

Inattentive listeners are seldom popular with peers or teachers, who are apt to categorize them as disinterested, uncaring, slow learning, or even rude. Teachers recognize those who do not or cannot listen by their repeated questions, requests for additional explanations, problems complying with oral directions, apparent disinterest, and inability to answer questions about listening content. Aside from teacher observation, very few tests or diagnostic techniques are currently available for planning specific instruction in listening.

Formal Detection

Unlike the tests in use 20 years ago that included measures of listening skills, only a few of the major standardized group-administered achievement test batteries currently in use contain listening measures. The types of skills surveyed are generally sentence completion or sentence comprehension and occasionally following oral directions. Listening abilities (or disabilities) are indirectly measured by a number of the other subtests that involve following the oral instructions of the examiner or the interpretation of oral content information.

Although the results of such testing tend to be nonspecific for instructional purposes, those that include direct measures of listening skills offer screening information. When the listening scores are substantially below scores on the other language arts subtests, then the need to observe and examine listening skills more thoroughly on an individual basis may be indicated.

Listening subtests are included as a part of some general speech and language tests and a few individually administered formal reading tests. Brief subtests of auditory memory frequently accompany tests of intellectual functioning. These test formats generally add important diagnostic data by permitting careful observation of the student's performance. Results of these tests are often used for classification purposes but seldom for academic instructional purposes.

Informal Detection

The most typical nonstandardized tests of listening are a variation of the informal reading inventory (IRI) format, containing sets of graded passages and questions used to determine a student's recall and interpretation of stories the examiner reads aloud. A student's performance of listening comprehension samples is intended for comparison with that student's oral or silent comprehension to gauge the gap, if any, between listening and independent reading. These are global measures that yield a general picture of students' abilities to remember the content of stories read to them.

Comparison of the results of both formal and informal testing, if available, with the listening demands of the curriculum can sometimes provide clues to listening needs. However, classroom observation alone often yields more valid as well as practical data. By first identifying the types of listening tasks a student needs to accomplish and then carefully observing that student's responses to those listening activities, you can derive a fairly accurate picture of the student's specific listening needs.

In the following chapters, the observable behaviors that are often demonstrated by students who have problems listening begin the discussion of each listening need (DETECTION). As indicated by the parenthetical references by skill number to related Special Needs (SN), many of the listening behaviors and skills are associated with each other and with reading skills. When several of these behaviors are exhibited consistently, you have reason to suspect a particular listening weakness. When confirmed during repeated observation and supported by oral and written responses and test scores, the instructional implications should be clear.

Easily distracted students often have difficulty listening for more than a few minutes, as do those who seem to need frequent movement for maximum concentration. Without strong listening skills, special learners are particularly at risk because their instructional interventions often involve numerous verbal explanations and the substitution of listening and speaking activities for reading or writing assignments.

CORRECTION OF SPECIAL LISTENING NEEDS

Listening difficulties interfere generally with classroom learning and specifically with growth in the language arts. The correction of listening needs can occur quickly with students who just need a few pointers or very slowly with students who are easily distracted or who have specific auditory deficits. Because critical listening requires sophisticated thinking skills, progress is often markedly slow. Corrective instruction should be provided on a daily basis for identified special needs, such as following oral directions or sequential recall. Additionally, students should be involved in listening-improvement experiences as a part of their studies in other subjects.

It is important to view the improvement of listening skills as both targeted instruction and integrated application. Unless they are used often and highlighted during other studies, listening skills will not transfer and become an established part of the student's learning strategy repertoire.

Beyond the individual topics treated in this section, certain general themes should be incorporated into the implementation of corrective listening instruction. Build or recall experiences related to the listening content with students prior to each listening activity. Because the language arts are mutually reinforcing, make an effort to provide concurrent or extension activities that also involve speaking, reading, and writing. Turn the students' listening needs into an opportunity to expose them to quality literature of various structures or concepts that they need to know. To guide the discussions of listening content, ask questions that require the listener to really think and teach the students to ask questions. Directly teach strategies such as self-questioning for students to monitor their listening comprehension. Adjust the length of the listening experiences to the needs of the students. Make listening an enjoyable experience by addressing students' interests, using varied visual props, adjusting lesson length to the needs of the students, and enjoying it yourself.

In addition to considering students' particular listening-skill needs, consult the teaching practices and CORRECTIVE PRINCIPLES in Part I for general guidelines that may apply to special learners. Then select and modify each CORRECTION strategy to match the specific learning needs of individual students.

1. ATTENDING TO AUDITORY STIMULI

DETECTION This may be a special skill need of students who:

- Attend to extraneous sounds and sights instead of listening activities
- Do not maintain eye contact while listening
- Consistently prefer visual to auditory stimuli
- Have difficulty discriminating sounds (SN 2)
- Do not follow oral directions (SN 5)
- Cannot recall the content of listening activities (SN 6–8)

Description. Some students appear to be better listeners than others. They respond more quickly to sounds and, on occasion, appear to prefer to use an auditory mode rather than a visual one. Attentive listening is no easy task in most classrooms. Students must be able to focus on the appropriate auditory stimuli to the exclusion of competing stimuli. Among the most common noises from outside the classroom are the sounds of teachers and students in adjacent rooms, students moving and talking in the halls, and students playing outside. From within a classroom, the sights and sounds of classmates and teachers can be even more distracting.

Causation. Inattention to specific auditory stimuli is a behavior typical of students who exhibit a general pattern of distractibility and/or high activity level. Classrooms that are too busy or too noisy make listening difficult for many students. Teachers who present boring or poorly planned lessons, demand that students sit very still while listening, or use material that is too easy or too difficult for the students cultivate inattention. Some students have never been coached to differentiate among sounds. Hearing deficits can interfere with attention and comprehension of various sounds. Special groups of students who may tend to exhibit inattentiveness are the culturally or language different, teacher disabled, behavior disordered, hearing impaired, language disabled, and learning disabled.

Implications. Attentive listening is an important learning skill. Throughout a school day, in every subject area, students are required to listen carefully. As a recognition-level experience, many students need training in attending to sounds prior to moving on to higher-level tasks involving differentiation, comprehension, and responding in a prescribed manner. Some students attend to groups of sounds without identifying their significance. Training in attending to sounds includes four types of auditory stimuli: human, nature, mechanical, and musical. Students should be taught to recognize, enjoy, and acknowledge sounds they hear around them but to selectively focus on the most important sound of the moment.

CORRECTION Modify these strategies to meet students' learning needs.

1. *Attention Helpers.* Some students need more or different types of help than others to focus their attention. Try one or more of these Attention Helpers: have students close their eyes while they listen; turn off the lights in the room; have them sit very still for brief intervals; tell them to try to see the source of the sound in their minds; give them a listening purpose; before listening, identify and discuss extraneous noises.
2. *Sound Imitations.* When a new sound is discovered or there is an old sound the students seem to like, have them try to make the sound. Duplicating sounds helps students to remember them and is an enjoyable experience.
3. *Noisy Books.* Check with the school librarian for titles of books that give special attention to sounds or noises. Read to the class and then, as you reread a story or passage, have the students listen and make the appropriate noises on cue. If the level of difficulty is appropriate, have the books available for students to read.
4. *Sound Seekers.* Send teams of students to the library, cafeteria, or office to sit quietly and listen to the number and types of sounds they can hear in a 5-minute period. Then have them report their findings by duplicating each sound they heard for peers to identify. Discuss why more sounds occur at certain times of the day. Have students repeat the procedures at home.
5. *Weather Sounds.* Take opportunities during or just before changes in the weather to have students listen for wind, rain, thunder, hail, and blowing leaves. View films or videotapes about weather for different storm sounds. Discuss the nature and implications of each sound.
6. *School Sounds.* As students begin to become aware of the many sounds around school, clarify the sources of the sounds. First have students watch as each noise is made. Footsteps, lawnmowers, the hum of the public address system, books closing, bells ringing, voices, and many more sounds fill the air. By learning to associate sounds with their origins, students will begin to learn the differences between kinds of sounds.
7. *Miniconcerts.* Two or three times a week, provide a 3–5 minute miniconcert for students to sit and listen to different types of music. Have them discuss how different types of music make them feel.
8. *Extra Practice.* • Have students tape sounds around school or home to share with others. • Ask students to bring tapes from home to share in school either in a listening center or during a miniconcert for the class. • Tape sounds from places such as the zoo, a farm, a busy street, or ballgame for students to guess the location and then identify the sounds.

2. DISCRIMINATING SOUNDS

DETECTION This may be a special skill need of students who:

- Cannot match similar sounds
- Do not distinguish subtle differences in sounds
- Confuse similar sounds
- Have difficulty attending to auditory stimuli (SN 1)
- Mispronounce certain letters and words (SN 21)

Description. Sound discrimination is a prerequisite skill for most language-related skills. Before identifying specific sounds, students must be able to discriminate among similar sounds. This involves not only recognizing similar sounds but also identifying subtle sound differences. The ability to differentiate general and spoken sounds precedes the discrimination of letter sounds, a skill vital to the mastery of phonetic analysis.

Causation. Many auditory discrimination errors are the direct result of students' inattention to the stimuli. Any type of hearing problem, regardless of source, can affect sound discrimination. Some students experience difficulty distinguishing sounds due to auditory-processing factors that may be neurologically based. Students who come from bilingual families or from homes in which oral and written language are not modeled and reinforced may also exhibit difficulties. Other groups of students who may exhibit auditory discrimination problems are the language disabled, learning disabled, and speech disordered.

Implications. Auditory discrimination is generally considered to be a speech skill and a reading readiness skill. Students who can already discriminate letter sounds probably will not need the more general types of experiences suggested for this skill. Students who require generalized practice in discriminating sounds can be taught individually or in listening centers. Because students tend to enjoy sound training, the global strategies for groups of students can be followed by more specific instruction that focuses on individual needs.

CORRECTION Modify these strategies to meet students' learning needs.

1. *Listening Tours.* Have students close their eyes and listen to the school sounds they hear. After 1–3 minutes, ask them to open their eyes and discuss the different sounds they heard. Lead a discussion by asking, "Which sound was the loudest? Which 2 sounds (if any) sounded the most alike? See if you can describe or imitate each sound." Later on, use several pretaped sounds and repeat the process.

2. *Sound Targets.* Teach students to focus on particular sounds to the exclusion of others. On days when the school is especially noisy, give them target sounds to listen for, such as what the teacher in the next room is saying. Secretly tape several students talking at the same time at lunch or on the playground; have the students identify the speakers and then repeat what a

target student said. Reinforce target listening by occasionally whispering a surprise or instructions to begin an enjoyable activity.

3. *Sound Sets.* Ask students to close their eyes or sit with their backs to you and listen to sets of sounds. Depending upon students' present skill level, these sound sets may be similar words or groups of school noises. After hearing each set, have students state if the sounds are alike or different. Begin by using very different sounds. Gradually move to more similar sounds. After students are able to distinguish similar sounds, begin using groups of 3 sounds and have students select the one that is different. You may need to take time after difficult sets of sounds to discuss how certain sounds differ or why students think some sounds are alike. Then repeat the same sounds to refocus student attention.

4. *Listening Rhymes.* Provide special times for students to participate in listening, singing, reading, and reciting different rhymes and linguistic-type reading materials. Most students love the flow and rhythm of rhyming literature and poetry. Begin by having students listen as you read stories or poetry. Follow up by having students sing a rhyming song. It is reinforcing if you can locate songs, stories, or poems that feature specific sound patterns that are or recently have been studied and applied in class. Using rhymes and Dr. Seuss–type books for listening, reading, and singing is an excellent means of exposing students to language and giving them a chance to hear and reproduce language patterns. Be sure to discuss the particular sounds that are highlighted in specific material so that students begin to distinguish different sounds.

5. *Word Contrasts.* When presenting new vocabulary or discussing specific words with students, take time to stress particularly troublesome phonemes and emphasize the correct sounds as they are made in each word. Have students repeat the words; after completing a lesson or explaining new words, go back again and have students pronounce each word. Ask students to listen for differences in the way specific words sound at the beginning or end.

6. *Word Families.* Present 2–3 additional words that sound like target words that appear in lessons. Target words may be new vocabulary or words that are particularly troublesome for students. By listing, pronouncing, discussing, and using these similar words in sentences, you are building both vocabulary and auditory discrimination skills.

7. *Extra Practice.* • Tape stories from linguistic readers for students to listen or read along. • Provide studysheets showing pairs of pictures; ask students to pronounce the name of each pictured object and then circle the ones that begin or end the same; repeat the procedure for picture names that differ. • Have students tape Sound Sets for peers to solve.

3. UNDERSTANDING SPECIFIC INFORMATION

DETECTION This may be a special skill need of students who:

- Frequently ignore oral comments
- Are unable to understand simple oral requests
- Do not appear to listen carefully (SN 1)
- Cannot discriminate among similar sounds (SN 2)
- Have difficulty following oral directions (SN 5)

Description. Understanding specific information requires students to listen and then either remember the information or carry out an action or request. During the course of a school day, students are expected to listen to assignments, explanations, directions, plans, and an assortment of other directives. Unfortunately, some students seem to ignore much of the oral information they receive. Listening involves hearing, processing, or thinking about the information and sometimes responding. Some experts refer to listening with understanding as *auding*.

Causation. The problems associated with inattentive listening and lack of understanding of specific information are often the result of poor listening habits or lack of motivation. Auditory discrimination difficulties interfere with understanding of auditory information. Students who are easily distracted may not listen long enough to extract needed information. Hearing deficits and language differences directly interfere with auditory comprehension. Other special groups of students who may experience difficulty include the behavior disordered, learning disabled, and speech disordered.

Implications. Most students can benefit from instruction to improve their auditory comprehension. The attention required to understand specific information could be compared to your response to the "beep, beep, beep" preceding a weather bulletin; you listen carefully for the type and location of the watch or warning. School-age students are often singled out for their apparent inattentive or selective listening that can contribute to miscommunications and misunderstandings. Not understanding information they hear causes students to miss much of the classroom instruction.

CORRECTION Modify these strategies to meet students' learning needs.

1. *Sight and Sound.* Have students think of something pleasant (e.g., a place, object, toy, or favorite activity) and the sounds they typically associate with it. Ask students to take turns stating what they see and hear in their minds by completing the statement "I see and hear . . ." Have each student repeat what previous students said and then add their visual and auditory images. If appropriate, have students imitate the sounds. As a variation, have students guess the object from descriptions of the sights and sounds.

2. *Sandy Says.* Use the first name of one of your students to play Simon Says. As the leader, you begin by saying, "Sandy says, 'Touch your nose. Wave to me.'" If the leader does not begin with "Sandy says," the students should not do as they are told. This helps students learn to listen for specific information. Have students take turns serving as leader and using their own names in the introductory statement.

3. *Misfits.* Read short stories or paragraphs to students. In each selection, include 1–2 items, actions, characters, or ideas that do not fit. Have students identify the misfits and explain why they are inaccurate. In early experiences, the misfit information should be easy to detect.

4. *Recitation.* Before a lesson, tell students that you will ask them to recall 1 important fact from the lesson. Then after completing a lesson, ask each of several students to tell you the 1 important fact or idea they remember. Several students should recall the same point. Discuss why each idea is important and why each student recalled the particular fact.

5. *Feedback.* After giving an assignment, routinely call on a student to repeat or explain the information again. It may surprise you how many students appear to listen but do not really understand what they have been asked to do. When students know that they are likely to be called upon to restate the information, they may attend more closely.

6. *Fact Finders.* To introduce a lesson, read the first page aloud. Ask students to listen for the most important facts as you read. After they have listened, ask students to tell you the most important facts they heard. Be sure to probe for additional information if an important fact is omitted. To extend the activity and build listening comprehension skills, have students use the important facts to predict the content of the lesson.

7. *Word Rhymes.* Form 2 teams. Have the first team provide a word and the second team name a word that rhymes with the first word. If successful, the first team must add a third rhyming word. When no more words can be named, the second team names a new word and the process continues. Award a point per correct word.

8. *Extra Practice.* • Appoint a class reporter for the day or week; assign the reporter to listen to radio or TV news broadcasts, recall or take notes on the key stories, and report back to the class. • Appoint a "Listening Leader" each day to listen to assignments and be available for other students to ask if a question comes up. • Ask students to record short unfinished stories or riddles on tape for peers; have different students listen to the information and respond back on a second tape by solving the riddle or providing an ending to the story. • Adapt strategies from Special Need 32.

4. UNDERSTANDING STANDARD SPOKEN ENGLISH

DETECTION This may be a special skill need of students who:

- Have trouble understanding Standard English
- Respond slowly when listening to Standard English
- Appear confused when hearing Standard English
- Have difficulty speaking Standard English (SN 18)

Description. Although standards for written English are readily available, standards for spoken English are not so carefully defined. Certain conventions are agreed upon as proper; however, pronunciation and even word order vary depending upon several factors that are loosely referred to as "dialectical or regional differences." Success in understanding oral communications is not so much mastery of specified skills as it is familiarity with specific language differences.

Causation. Students' cultural and language differences are the main causes of their inability to understand Standard American English. Understanding different versions of English is largely a matter of practice and exposure. The closer the match with the student's own oral language, the better the student's understanding. Some students and teachers have had little exposure to a Mexican-American language pattern or to the language of a particular region. Students whose cultural and language backgrounds differ from those of the school are particularly handicapped by even a slight hearing loss. Although other special groups of students may have difficulty understanding what they hear, their problems tend to be more general rather than confined to Standard English.

Implications. Much as parents learn to understand a child's invented or developing language, many students learn to understand language that is sometimes altered by numerous factors. To some degree, the standards set by the language used in national news broadcasts are the functional standards for spoken English. However, in most instances, the standard or level of correctness is determined by the language context within the classroom, school, and city in which teachers and students live. Thus, for academic success, students must master the standard English of the particular school they attend.

CORRECTION Modify these strategies to meet students' learning needs.

1. *Patterned Literature.* Select poetry and stories that reflect a patterned style of writing. Such writing includes predictable patterns of usage, such as rhyming words and recurring parts. Have students listen, repeat each line after you, or, if possible, participate in choral reading to gain both a feel and an understanding of the language. Place tapes of such stories at a listening center for students to independently listen to or read along.

2. *Creative Conversations.* Expose students to situations in which they must use and understand standard English in conversation between 1–4 students. Using personal language is a relaxed means of learning to understand language. Provide students with interesting topics, ranging from new music, food, or sports events to school activities. Emphasize enunciation and the importance of looking at people when they speak.

3. *Reality Roles.* Have students roleplay shopping in a grocery, book, or record store. To begin, the teacher should be the store clerk and encourage use of language for products and money transactions. Initially, use visual props to facilitate comprehension, but eliminate the visuals as students progress.

4. *Picture Talks.* Give students interesting pictures and have them describe what is happening in the picture. Use small groups and encourage the listeners to ask questions to help the speaker clarify the descriptions. Model the process several times before having students begin their Picture Talks. Students having difficulty should listen to tapes of the picture descriptions before presenting their talk.

5. *Multicultural Literature.* It is important to use literature that reflects the varied cultural backgrounds of students. Use folktales, stories, and songs that highlight the cultural background of each of your students. If necessary, contact some of the parents or local librarians to assist you in finding representative literature for the cultural groups in your class. Use this literature as you would any other. Exposure to literature of different cultures will make some students feel more comfortable and help other students learn more about their classmates.

6. *Listening Links.* Give students specific purposes for listening to a story, poem, or story part. For example, tell students to "Listen for the names of the 3 sisters," "See if you can figure out where the twins live," "Decide how many good things happened to the hero in this story," or "Listen to find how the 2 players felt after the game." Such purposes simplify the task of the listeners and help focus their attention on important points. The purposes are an aid to linking understanding with listening.

7. *Extra Practice.* • Encourage students to bring their own pictures to class for use in Picture Talks. • Peer teaching is recommended to reinforce language instruction whenever possible. • Plan read-alongs involving 2 students who read together (choral reading) to a small group of younger students. • Record portions of radio or television broadcasts and have students listen and then write down the major stories or key ideas from the 2–3-minute excerpts. • For additional activities, adapt the ones suggested for Special Needs 18 and 20.

5. FOLLOWING ORAL DIRECTIONS

DETECTION This may be a special skill need of students who:

- Do not follow oral directions
- Frequently ask that directions be repeated
- Have difficulty attending to auditory stimuli (SN 1)
- Have trouble understanding oral directions (SN 3)
- Often forget auditory information (SN 6)
- Confuse the sequence of oral directions (SN 7)

Description. For instructional purposes, there are at least two levels of of oral directions. The first level is one of general awareness, wherein students are expected to gain an overall understanding of one or two directives. A second, more difficult level involves students in both understanding directions and then making some decision as to how or where to begin a specified action or response. Problems with this second level are apparent in the behavior of those students who seem to understand what is stated but then become confused once they attempt to carry out an assignment.

Causation. One reason that students may have trouble following oral directions is that the instructions may not be clearly stated. Teachers sometimes assume that because the information is intelligible to them, it is equally understandable to students. When too many directions are given at once or when teachers are too hurried, vague, or brief in supplying the information required for tasks to be accomplished, even the best students have difficulty. Some students are unable to attend and concentrate long enough to understand what is being said. Auditory problems of a physical or processing nature can also restrict students' understanding. Other special groups of learners who may exhibit difficulty complying with directions are the behavior disordered, hearing impaired, language disabled, and learning disabled.

Implications. Many teachers consider compliance with oral directions to be a prerequisite skill for survival in school. Students who require repeated coaching and explanations are often considered to be a problem. In some instances, teachers do not accept the responsibility for providing accurate and clearly stated directions. For students who experience learning difficulties, careful directions and explanations or examples of completed assignments are even more important. Lengthy instructions should be broken into manageable steps and accompanied by visual cues. In many cases, students do not realize until after the fact that they do not understand directions. Keeping a continual watch is important for the correction of misunderstandings as students go about completing assigned work.

CORRECTION Modify these strategies to meet students' learning needs.

1. *Word Signals.* Have students listen for the key words or Word Signals that tell them what to do. To demonstrate, have them do whatever they are told the minute they hear it. Emphasize the key words as you say, for example, "*Stand* up," "*Turn* around," "*Touch* your *desk*," or "*Pick up* your *pencil.*" Then discuss the words that signal what to do in written assignments: "*Circle* the word that *matches* each *picture.*" Emphasize the word signals each time you give oral instructions. Gradually increase the length and complexity of the directions as students progress.

2. *Direction Distractors.* When giving oral directions, insert 1–2 unnecessary words or steps. Recognize or reward students who first identify the distractors. List directions for assignments on the board and include 1–2 unnecessary comments. Have students listen as you read aloud directions. Then ask students to identify the distracting information.

3. *Forced Recall.* Begin with simple directions for an in-class assignment or homework. Ask students to restate the directions to a classmate. Have the student receiving the information confirm or clarify the accuracy of the restatement. Then have a student restate the directions to the class to be sure that all understand.

4. *Dispersing Directions.* Ask students who appear to be having difficulty understanding oral directions to serve as work coordinators. Before stating directions, meet with 1–2 coordinators to explain and demonstrate what is to be done. Then explain the work to the class, allowing the coordinators to hear the directions again. If students have questions as work begins, they should contact a coordinator. Coordinators may ask each other to clarify concerns. When uncertain, coordinators should ask the teacher.

5. *Elaborated Explanations.* Give students directions that lack sufficient information to complete assigned tasks. Encourage students to ask questions to force you to provide more information. List the additional information students request on the board. If needed, give 2 sets of directions and have students decide which is the most helpful and why.

6. *Extra Practice.* • Give students an oral list of 2–4 items to be completed; then have them go to a small group and explain the information and answer any questions. • Select student leaders and have them lead the class as they all listen to tapes of directions that require students to make sound effects or gestures. • Adapt ideas from Special Needs 6 and 7.

6. REMEMBERING GENERAL INFORMATION

DETECTION This may be a special skill need of students who:

- Do not remember the content of listening experiences
- Have difficulty listening for more than a few minutes
- Are easily distracted while listening (SN 1)
- Have problems understanding what they hear (SN 3)
- Do not follow oral directions (SN 5)

Description. Remembering the general content of listening experiences includes understanding major concepts, main ideas, inferences, and information associated with a central topic. Not only are students expected to remember the content of oral directions, but they must also recall oral explanations, rules, deadlines, requests, homework, and the like. Most teachers permit but do not necessarily encourage students to write down their homework assignments or take notes for the important information.

Causation. Poor concentration, fatigue, neurological problems, low mental ability, disorganized presentations of oral information, and a general lack of effort can interfere with students' retention of the general information presented as a listening experience. Among the special groups of students who may experience difficulty are the teacher disabled, behavior disordered, language disabled, learning disabled, mentally retarded, and slow learners.

Implications. Students who continually misinterpret or forget general information experience embarrassment and poor achievement and sometimes begin to develop avoidance behaviors. Remembering oral information requires careful attention to words and gestures as well as asking for clarification at the appropriate time during lesson presentation, not after independent work has begun. Some teachers merely threaten or remind students to listen carefully. Many students need direct practice remembering information, practice that can be easily integrated with subject-area lessons. Training can benefit many students by helping them establish a routine or pattern of behavior that assists in understanding, organizing, and remembering oral information.

CORRECTION Modify these strategies to meet students' learning needs.

1. *Setting Purposes.* Prior to every listening task, give students a purpose for listening. Before reading a section from a textbook to the class, ask them to listen for certain information. After listening is completed, ask students to state what they remember, based upon the purposes you stated. Following a similar procedure, have students listen to tapes to accomplish 1 or more purposes. As students progress, have them set their own purposes for listening.
2. *Misinformation.* Give students 2–4 facts or general concepts from material they will be hearing. One of the pieces of information should be left out or not make sense. If required, list the information on the board and review it orally before beginning the listening experience. While you read aloud the passage, have students listen and decide what does not fit in the paragraph or short selection. Then discuss why the misinformation does not fit.
3. *Sentence Completion.* Periodically stop in midsentence while discussing material with students. Encourage students to complete your statement. Reward those whose answers are logical, thereby keeping them alert for opportunities to help out and demonstrate their attentiveness.
4. *Quizmates.* Ask students to listen to material being read aloud by you or on tape. Provide a list of questions orally or for students to read before listening. After listening, have students work in pairs, asking and answering the questions. If one pair of students does not know an answer, have them consult with another pair of peers. As an extension activity, have students develop additional questions that could be asked about the passage.
5. *Class Profiles.* Make an audiotape of each student talking or reading aloud. Have students close their eyes and listen as you describe someone in the room. Then play the tape of the chosen person talking. Ask students to guess who the person is and what information supports their choice.
6. *Musical Moods.* After studying particular topics in reading, literature, science, or history, play 2–3 different musical recordings and have students decide which one best fits the mood of the material. Have each student justify his or her choice. As a variation, have students select music to accompany particular passages.
7. *Logical Facts.* Give students 3–5 pieces of information about an event or story. After they hear the information, ask students to work alone or in teams to decide what happened or what event is being described. If possible, have students organize the information in sequence. Students who want to take notes should be encouraged to do so but only after the brief listening material has been presented, not while the information is being stated.
8. *Extra Practice.* • Provide 2–5-minute listening adventures on audiotapes; have students listen to the material and then write or retell the story to a friend. • As a follow-up or review, give students 2–6 questions about a particular topic; have them listen to a tape of you or a peer reading aloud a chapter or section and answer the questions. • Tape a descriptive message in which you or a student describe the major characteristics of a common object; after listening, have students write down what they think is being described. Check the answers and reward best guesses and correct responses. • Adapt strategies from Special Needs 3 and 5.

7. RECALLING INFORMATION IN SEQUENCE

DETECTION This may be a special skill need of students who:

- Cannot remember oral information in sequence
- Recall the facts but not in order
- Remember only a few details
- Forget much of what they hear (SN 6)
- Have difficulty following oral directions (SN 5)

Description.   Sequential recall after listening is a skill commonly associated with the content areas of science, social studies, and mathematics. Recalling information in sequence requires students to understand the content and then organize their thinking to store the information in a manner that allows for sequential retrieval. The typical classroom task presented to young students, however, is the recall of general information, with little emphasis on sequence. Aside from following oral directions to complete assignments, there is usually little opportunity and no real need to sequentially recall information until a heavy emphasis is placed upon content-area subjects.

Causation.   Demonstration, organization, and meaningful practice are necessary for most students to maintain sequential recall. Certain individuals tend to be patterned and organized in their daily activities; these students will probably find it easy to recall information sequentially. Because understanding the general information of listening activities is prerequisite to sequential recall of the content, any interference with comprehension of content also interferes with sequential recall. Special students who may tend to either forget or confuse sequence are those with hearing, language, or learning disabilities.

Implications.   Problems recalling information in sequence are usually not noticed until the middle grade levels, when students are involved in experiments, extensive timelines, and mathematical formulae requiring specified procedures. Sequential order seems to be an easier task for some students than others. Most students can benefit from specific training to improve their sequential recall of auditory information. As adults, sequential recall is not required as often as recall of general information, depending upon one's job or daily activities. Sequential recall is, then, a very specialized skill. Unless students are required to sequentially recall information for legitimate purposes and on a regular basis, the need for corrective instruction may be limited to improving skills for following oral directions.

CORRECTION Modify these strategies to meet students' learning needs.

1. *Concept Completion.* After listening to a selection or story, have students listen to 1–2 additional facts not stated in the passage. Discuss the importance of each fact to understanding the content. Then ask the students to decide where the information should be placed in the story. Reread the passage with the new information inserted to confirm the sequence; rearrange as needed.

2. *Postlistening Strips.* After reading aloud a passage, give pairs or small groups of students sentence strips about the major events. On each strip, write 1–2 sentences; for beginning readers, use rebuses for the difficult words. Have students read their sentences aloud and then decide the order in which the sentences must be arranged to retell the passage. Discuss the logic of the placement of each sentence.

3. *Prelistening Strips.* Use the sentence strips as in the above activity, but present them before reading aloud a passage. Have students read aloud their sentences and arrange them in logical order to predict the passage content. After you read aloud the passage, have students reread the sentences to rearrange or confirm the proper sequence.

4. *Memory Sequence.* Read aloud scrambled sentences. Ask students to sort each sentence and say the words in the correct order. Since there often are several ways to sequence the words in a sentence, discuss the possibilities and decide on the best order. As students progress, have them retell and then rewrite each sentence in order.

5. *Musical Events.* Ask students to listen to carefully selected music to determine, according to the lyrics, the order of events in specific songs. Then have them tell the story of each song in correct sequence.

6. *Recipes.* Many students are interested in how things are put together. Cooking, experiments, models, and related tasks require things to be constructed or assembled in a definite order. Orally explain a recipe for a simple food or item that can be built. Show the value of doing things in proper sequence. Illustrate, with student assistance, what happens if the correct sequence is not followed.

7. *Daily Events.* To emphasize the role of sequence in daily events, have students listen for the sequence of presentation for such events as TV programs, the school day, lunchtime, or after-school events. For example, most local newscasts follow a sequence of news, sports, and weather. Discuss the value of sequence and why events are sequenced as they are.

8. *Extra Practice.* • Send out sequence hunters to watch for things that appear to happen at certain times (e.g., noon whistles, traffic lights, trains); have students describe their findings. • Ask students to listen for sounds that either follow or precede certain events, such as thunder or a knock at the door; have students report back to the class. • Adapt strategies from Special Needs 5 and 6.

8. LISTENING CRITICALLY

DETECTION This may be a special skill need of students who:

- Cannot evaluate the content of listening experiences
- Accept what they are told at face value
- Understand surface meanings only
- Display generally weak auditory memory skills (SN 5–7)
- Are not critical readers (SN 34)

Description.   Critical listening requires students to evaluate the worth, validity, and message of information they hear. Responding to auditory information and making decisions are tasks that require students to think, pay careful attention, and make comparative judgments. Listeners must understand the general information and then interpret the language and sometimes the nonverbal cues. They must also listen for what is not said. Listening for bias, mood, embedded meaning, or underlying feelings requires students to pay special attention to ways in which information is stated. A valuable precursor to critical reading, critical listening involves the higher levels of cognitive processing.

Causation.   Both problem-solving functions and higher-order mental functions are involved in evaluative listening. A lack of practice and training are responsible for some students' inabilities to listen and make evaluative decisions. Other students are hampered by difficulty thinking beyond a literal level. Without extensive outside knowledge and experiences, students have little by which to judge what they hear. Critical listening is an especially difficult task for many special learners in all categories.

Implications.   Critical listening is evaluative listening, or what some teachers call "listening with a third ear." Most students can become better listeners and, to some extent, learn to listen critically. At some point, however, specific thinking, problem-solving, and reasoning skills will be needed to successfully evaluate information. Instruction must often begin with concrete examples and operations before moving into more abstract reasoning or evaluative types of problems. Students must also develop or be taught criteria by which to judge information. The thinking strategies, meaningful practice, and criteria to judge content improve students' abilities to be active, thinking listeners as well as critical readers.

CORRECTION Modify these strategies to meet students' learning needs.

1. *Rating Rules.* Guide students to develop sets of rules for evaluating listening content. Begin with very simple ones for differentiating fact from fiction. Talk through the process of analyzing obvious statements, such as "Alison's face is green" or "Angel flew to the top of the building," and move to groups of statements and then to passages. As students progress, develop similar rules for rating such elements as quality, style, mood, and purpose of listening exercises.

2. *Fact or Not?* Read to students statements that require them to decide if the information is fact or opinion. Take statements from subject matter previously covered in daily lessons. Use or develop rules to judge the statements and passages. Guide students to restate facts as opinions and opinions as facts.

3. *Emotives.* Read a paragraph aloud that contains several emotional words; then read a paragraph about the same topic but without the emotional words. Ask students to decide which reading gets the point across the best or which is most convincing. Explain how the use of certain words plus the speaker's tone and gestures affect the way we receive information. Then have students reword the paragraph for different audiences. To extend the concepts, have students listen to advertisements to identify emotional words and their effects.

4. *Real-Life Judgments.* Prerecord segments from popular television shows that take place in a courtroom. Use 1–2-minute segments and have students watch and listen to determine which attorney, witness, or plaintiff sounds the most prepared, accurate, excited, at fault, nervous, and so on. Discuss what the characters said and did that helped students make their judgments.

5. *Editorial Bias.* Read aloud 2–3 letters to the editor that address the same topic. Ask students to determine which one states the strongest case. Have students justify their answers. Then have them suggest ways to strengthen the other letters.

6. *Notable News.* Have students develop weekly news reports about events that occur in the community or school. Guide students to present their information in a manner that is slanted or biased. Ask peers to listen to the stories and discuss which ones they liked or believed and why. Then discuss ways to improve each story.

7. *Irrelevant Information.* Read sections to students from their history, science, or reading textbooks. In each paragraph, include 1–2 unrelated statements or pieces of information. Pause after each paragraph, and ask students to identify the irrelevant information and tell why it does not fit.

8. *Extra Practice.* • Have students audiotape 2 1-minute commercials for a product of their choice; the commercials can both be positive, both negative, or 1 positive and 1 negative. Have peers listen to both commercials and decide if they are positive or negative and tell why. • Tape articles from one of the weekly newspapers that specializes in sensationalism; have students listen to evaluate the content. • Adapt suggestions from Special Need 34.

9. ENJOYING BEING READ TO

DETECTION This may be a special skill need of students who:

- Show little interest in being read to
- Seem restless while being read to
- Appear inattentive during listening activities (SN 1)
- Display generally weak auditory memory skills (SN 5–8)

Description. Reading to children is one of the most important acts a parent or teacher can offer, particularly for young or struggling readers. Most students, regardless of age, enjoy or can learn to enjoy listening to someone read. Good literature, read in a meaningful manner, can be a pleasurable experience for both the reader and listener. Reading materials should be interesting and selection can be a joint decision, self-selected by students, or chosen by teachers.

Causation. Students who do not enjoy being read to have probably either had negative listening experiences, have a hearing or attention deficit of some type, or perhaps have never really had the opportunity to sit and listen to an interesting reader with a good book. Widespread use of television as an entertainment source and student participation in multiple after-school activities often leave little time for listening to a good book. In homes where parents read and have books available, the children are more likely to become interested in books and reading. Teachers who are unenthusiastic or too rigid in their presentations take the fun out of listening. Among the groups of students who may need to be taught the joys of being read to are the disadvantaged, culturally or language different, teacher disabled, behavior disordered, hearing impaired, language disabled, and learning disabled.

Implications. The emphasis should be on enjoyment and discussion when reading aloud to students. Until they begin to enjoy the activities, use guided discussions to reinforce concepts and encourage active listening, rather than directly quiz the students about the content. The teacher who is enthusiastic about the presentation transmits enjoyment. When choosing passages to read, the length of the selections should be matched to the listeners' attention span, using the best literature available. For younger students, books that have received the Caldecott Medal (for the top picture book) or the Newbery Medal (for the top children's book) make excellent choices. Students who learn to enjoy hearing someone read are more likely to become good listeners and readers themselves. In addition to enjoyment, other goals of reading to students are to improve general language skills, encourage interest in books, and create a desire to read.

CORRECTION Modify these strategies to meet students' learning needs.

1. *Understandable Fun.* Present each read-aloud activity as a positive, fun experience, not just another lesson. Permit students to lounge or get comfortable. Begin with simple and short stories that are easily understood and are humorous or rhythmical. Read with enthusiasm and expression; ham it up and enjoy yourself! Your involvement and enjoyment will be contagious. Occasionally ask students to predict what they think will happen next. After reading, ask the students to tell you what they did and did not like about the story; then use their preferences to select the next story.

2. *Book Talks.* Strictly speaking, Book Talks should not replace reading to students. However, since so many excellent books are available, to expose students to as many as possible, select a few that are written on a level that the listeners can read independently. Give a brief overview of each and read aloud several interesting sections. Then tell students where to find these books to read in their entirety.

3. *Musical Affects.* When it can be matched to the theme or to particular portions of a book you are sharing with your students, play instrumental music softly in the background. Music that is not too distracting and is kept at a low volume can complement the story and add to enjoyment. For some books, it may be appropriate to play a recording for 2–3 minutes to set the mood before reading. And some special music, such as ballads or folk songs, can be shared with students after reading.

4. *Classroom Libraries.* Have plenty of good books available in class. Although it is usually best to finish books you begin reading to a class, try giving special previews of particularly good books. If books are readily available in class, students are more likely to use them. Introduce special authors of theme books by reading aloud only 1 book of a series. Follow up by having similar books available in class or reserved in the school library.

5. *Recommended Books.* In addition, your librarian's recommendations, consult the following sources of reviews and discussions about good literature for children: *Childhood Education, The Horn Book Magazine, Instructor,* and *Language Arts.* With so many good books available, why not select the best to teach students the joys of books?

6. *Extra Practice.* • Send letters home recommending good choices of books for birthdays and other gifts. • Schedule a time for students to read portions of books to younger students. • Encourage parents to take students to the public library for storytimes. • Adapt suggestions from Special Needs 10 and 30.

10. ENJOYING DIFFERENT LISTENING EXPERIENCES

DETECTION This may be a special skill need of students who:

- Are familiar with only one read-aloud format
- Have attended few plays or concerts
- Have seldom heard a live speech or poetry reading
- Do not seem to enjoy being read to (SN 9)

Description. The types of listening skills and appreciations that students develop are dependent in part on the kinds of listening activities to which they are exposed. Different types of listening experiences offer different understandings and concepts. Although the read-aloud story format is the one most often used with young children, the addition of a variety of listening experiences aids students to develop the schema with which to understand the many types of speaking, reading, and writing formats they will encounter in language interactions. Exposure to a variety of text structures as well as to plays, concerts, readings, debates, speeches, and parades can increase students' interest in and mastery of the language arts.

Causation. Many students have not been exposed to a variety of listening events. For disadvantaged youngsters from homes of limited education, finances, and/or adult attention, television is often the primary source of listening and artistic involvement. Unfortunately, the types of programming that educational stations provide is often not what students choose to watch on a regular basis. Teachers often rely on the read-aloud narrative story as the only means of developing listening appreciation and enjoyment, exposing students to the single text structure and listening format. In addition to those who lack a broad base of general experiences, the groups of students who may need to be taught the joys of a variety of listening experiences, including being read to, are the disadvantaged, culturally or language different, teacher disabled, behavior disordered, hearing impaired, language disabled, and learning disabled.

Implications. Many students and adults, as well, seem content with familiar experiences and the known world. Changes or differences in people, places, and forms of entertainment sometimes produce discomfort and insecurity. Unless youngsters experience a variety of literary forms and events, their potential enjoyment as well as future career opportunities may be limited. There is no reason to attempt to enforce or expect students to enjoy all the new experiences they encounter. However, exposure to a variety of language forms is necessary to enable students to learn what they like or do not like. Even participation in activities that students do not like builds a frame of reference and experience to use in understanding future language experiences.

CORRECTION Modify these strategies to meet students' learning needs.

1. *Reformatted Stories.* Frequently vary the type and presentation style of traditional read-aloud stories. Always give the listeners a purpose. Alternate different types of stories, using fables, fairytales, science fiction, archaic language, modern language, fact, fiction, and even entertaining advertisements. Read a fairytale and then retell or have the students retell it as a modern realistic story. Read a fable and then retell it as a modern-day story, using your students as the characters. As you read aloud, show pictures, transparencies, or flannelboard figures; use gestures; speak each character's part in a different voice; assign students to act out characters as you read; or have students make the special sound effects as they listen.

2. *Tape Critique.* Play taped stories or expository passages. Think aloud as you interpret, predict, and then critique the passage content. After you model the process several times, have students join in to critique listening experiences. To vary the activity as well as assist students to develop listening preferences, think aloud what you like or do not like about a passage and explain why. After modeling, have students join in.

3. *Personal Profiles.* Most communities include people who either are currently or have been involved in entertainment in college or as professionals. Invite such resource speakers to visit your class to explain, demonstrate, or share costumes or pictures about their area of expertise. Visits by local writers, reporters, singers, or musicians can bring a touch of personal realism to auditory experiences. Students may also develop a greater respect for the effort involved in creating certain events.

4. *Classroom Productions.* Have students put on a simple 1-act play and experience the details required in staging, acting, and sound effects. Consult your basal reader or librarian for sources of appropriate plays.

5. *Recorded Presentations.* Excellent tapes of plays, poetry readings, dramatic readings, and the like are available in most school and public libraries. Select a variety of such tapes to present in class 1 day a week. Preview the tapes so you can interpret the content and establish appropriate listening purposes. After students have listened for a specific purpose, have them listen a second time to critique the content, as in Activity 2.

6. *Comparative Reviews.* Use newspaper reviews of movies, concerts, and plays and have students determine what might be good choices. Use reviews from old papers and share them with students for movies they have seen. Discuss how such differences in taste can occur.

7. *Extra Practice.* • Ask your students to attend and review a concert or play for the class. • Carefully select acceptable tapes of popular music to place at a listening center for students' listening pleasure. • Use the entertainment sections from newspapers for students to plan a weekend of entertainment and justify their choices.

REFLECTIONS

1. The introductory discussion to Part II presents a general overview of special listening needs. Now that you have read about each of the skills, what additional points would you emphasize or clarify in the introduction? Why?

2. The special listening needs in Part II are organized according to three general areas: attentive listening, auditory memory, and auditory appreciation. Review reading and language texts in a learning resource center or curriculum library. Compare and contrast the skills listed in these materials with the ones cited in this section. Which listening areas receive the most attention? Why? Which ones should receive more emphasis? Why?

3. Various listening skills are described in the first paragraph of the discussion of each Special Need. With a particular group of students in mind, reread these descriptions to decide which listening skills are the most important to successful academic functioning in most subjects. Then rank-order Special Needs 1–10 according to their relative importance.

4. Some of the observable behaviors that signal problems in a particular listening skill are listed at the beginning of the discussion of each skill. Select one of the three major areas (attention, memory, appreciation); list the DETECTION behaviors for that section. Then observe in a regular classroom to detect these behaviors. Record any additional problem behaviors that you observe, and then ask peers to add to the list. Next observe in a special education classroom and follow similar procedures.

5. CORRECTIVE PRINCIPLES for categories of special students are presented in Part I. Select a real or hypothetical special learner with an identified listening need. Use the teaching practices in Chapter 1 and the CORRECTIVE PRINCIPLES in Chapters 2 and 3 as guidelines to select and modify the CORRECTION listening strategies to meet the probable learning needs of the selected student.

6. Listening is a major vehicle for teaching language skills and for explaining concepts and mechanics in all subjects. Observe in a regular classroom and in a special education class, noting the types of listening exercises and determining the amount of time students are engaged in listening activities. Compare and contrast your findings in the two settings and then explain any differences.

7. Different learners can tolerate various types and amounts of distractions. Consider the circumstances under which you can best listen, and then design a classroom to maximize your listening attention and comprehension. What adjustments would be required for special learners? Why?

8. Listening lessons must be carefully planned to meet the specific learning needs of special students. Plan two or more such listening lessons for a special learner. To design your lessons, use the diagnostic information available from the school, lesson content that matches the learner's skill needs and interests, the teaching practices in Chapter 1, and the CORRECTIVE PRINCIPLES to guide the selection and modification of one or more of the CORRECTION strategies for each listening need.

9. Implementation of special lessons often includes adjustments during teaching. Practice the listening lessons you designed for the special learner with a peer. Then teach those lessons to the special learner, modifying your plans according to the student's needs as you teach.

10. Several language arts books present some suggestions for teaching listening skills to a variety of learners. Compare and contrast discussions in these sources with the information in Chapters 4–6:

Bromley, K. D. (1988). *Language arts: Exploring connections*. Boston: Allyn and Bacon.

Hennings, D. G. (1986). *Communication in action: Teaching the language arts* (3rd ed.). Boston: Houghton Mifflin.

Hoskisson, K., & Tompkins, G. E. (1987). *Language arts: Content and teaching strategies*. Columbus, OH: Charles E. Merrill.

Norton, D. E. (1985). *The effective teaching of language arts* (2nd ed.).Columbus, OH: Charles E. Merrill.

Petty, W. T., Petty, D. C., & Becking, M. F. (1985). *Experiences in language: Tools and techniques for language arts methods* (4th ed.). Boston: Allyn and Bacon.

Tiedt, S. W., & Tiedt, I. M. (1987). *Language arts activities for the classroom* (2nd ed.). Boston: Allyn and Bacon.

Trelease, J. (1985). *The read-aloud handbook*. New York: Viking Penguin.

Wallace, G., Cohen, S. B., & Polloway, E. A. (1987). *Language arts: Teaching exceptional students*. Austin, TX: Pro-Ed.

PART III

SPECIAL SPEAKING NEEDS

As speaking is our primary means of communication, speaking skills are a basic requirement for learning and demonstrating knowledge in all areas. The developmental sequence of the language arts progresses from listening to speaking before reading and writing. In order to learn to speak naturally, students must first be able to listen and comprehend language. Unlike listening, which involves the decoding of information that is received, speaking is an encoding task in which the speaker orally expresses ideas. Although most students enter school with some oral language facility, they must expand these skills in order to progress academically.

Speaking plays an important role in students' academic progress as well as in their social success. Nonetheless, speaking like listening is often slighted in curricular plans in favor of other subjects. The tendency of the schools to overlook the deliberate improvement of speaking skills is probably the result of three inter-related factors: 1) Teachers take speaking for granted because most students have already developed oral language skills when they enter school; 2) teachers view instruction in the more traditional subjects as their teaching mission; and 3) teachers typically are not required to grade their students in speaking as a subject. When speaking is graded, it usually appears in the conduct column of the progress report as "does not participate" or "talks too much."

The speaking skills in Part III are categorized as either oral expression or speech. The skills discussed in Chapter 7 are generally considered to be oral language skills; these are distinct from but related to the speech skills of Chapter 8. Thus, the topics discussed as oral expression are the more typical language arts treatments of recognizing and correcting problems associated with speaking. Included are acquiring, generating, and using oral language, questioning, presenting and discussing, social amenities and creative dramatics.

The information provided in Chapter 8, "Speech," is more specialized than what is sometimes seen in a language arts text. We include the common speech difficulties that are often exhibited by special students. This chapter focuses on linguistic differences, speech anxiety, various forms of presentation, and those speech disorders traditionally considered to be the domain of the speech pathologist: articulation, voice, and fluency. The inclusion of the speech disorders is not intended to tread on the turf of the speech specialists but rather to supplement their services.

DETECTION OF SPECIAL SPEAKING NEEDS

Teachers should not be expected to act as speech diagnosticians. They should, however, have a general idea of when students require evaluation by a speech pathologist. A nontechnical but useful determiner is to refer students when their speech causes you to listen to *how they talk* rather than *what they say*. Oral language is a very complex process that can best be evaluated by a licensed speech pathologist.

Formal Detection

Unlike listening, oral language is not a part of formal group-administered achievement testing but is tested on an individual basis by specially trained clinicians. Such testing is frequently conducted as a part of the evaluation of students who are suspected of being handicapped or of the reevaluation of those previously identified. The individually administered speech/language tests generally include measures of both receptive or decoding elements and expressive or encoding elements and may involve several different test sources. The results usually indicate the mastery of certain language structures but not what or how to plan instruction accordingly.

Informal Detection

One of the most logical informal detection strategies is the use of the language experience approach, wherein students are provided with an experience or asked to recall one and then tell about it. As you record the retellings on tape or in writing, you can readily note a student's specific speech patterns as well as the use of semantics and syntax. As an added bonus, the students' stories can later be used to teach reading and writing. Other informal diagnostic strategies involve a similar analysis of students' oral responses to questions, their descriptions of objects and events, or their conversations and discussions.

Some of the behaviors that are indicative of specific speaking problems are listed at the beginning of the discussion of each Special Need. Behaviors related to other language skills are parenthethically noted. Many students, particularly those who are chronologically or intellectually young, demonstrate some of these errors from time to time. When these errors form a behavior pattern that is consistently demonstrated in daily oral language interactions, a special need is indicated. Even if the need is so mild as to preclude the services of a speech pathologist, you have probably detected a logical point to begin corrective instruction.

The causes of speaking problems range from sensory to physical and intellectual, often including environmental differences. Lack of sufficient language stimulation or experience often contributes to deficits. Students who are hearing impaired or cerebral palsied or who have cleft palates tend to exhibit multiple communication disorders. Evidence suggests that more girls than boys may exhibit communication disorders and that articulation problems are more likely to occur in children who are from low socioeconomic areas, have low intelligence levels, and are not firstborn children. A number of different types of special students also exhibit difficulties speaking.

CORRECTION OF SPECIAL SPEAKING NEEDS

Speaking difficulties are apt to interfere with reading and written expression, particularly when language comprehension is involved. Words and text that have not been first mastered at the listening and speaking levels are not likely to be read or written with skill and understanding. Although speech disorders themselves need not disrupt progression in reading or writing, the auditory-processing deficits that often accompany speech disorders may create specific problems in word recognition and spelling.

Most students can benefit from instruction to improve their speaking skills, their primary means of communication, without requiring enrollment in speech and language therapy. The teacher's role in enhancing oral language includes not only providing the targeted instruction but also serving as a proper speaking model. Even those students who participate in speech therapy can benefit from supplementary classroom instruction if it is directed by the speech pathologist and coordinated with the speech and language program.

In these chapters, the strategies for correcting problems of articulation, voice, stuttering, language formulation, speech anxiety, and presentation forms are general enough in nature to be adapted for use with students experiencing less

severe speech difficulties. When teaching students who are linguistically different, a forced change in dialect is seldom a reasonable or attainable goal. Efforts to
alter student dialects or nonstandard speech are more effective when less direct
methods are used. By modeling, applying, and encouraging alternate usage
students' adaptations are likely to increase.

To be effective, corrective instruction must include ample meaningful speaking opportunities that involve interactions of all types. Structure speaking activities and integrate them throughout the curriculum. Carefully manipulate the
speaker's audience so that the environment is a safe and supportive one. Use
students' language and experiences as the foundation upon which to build additional language and experiences. Model the organization of ideas to speak; have
students follow your model; and teach oral language as a thinking skill. Provide
positive corrective feedback as needed by casually repeating correctly the idea
the student attempts to express. Orally label and describe objects and events
and encourage students to do likewise. Consult your speech and language
pathologist often for guidance and for special tips.

For general guidelines for selecting strategies to teach identified special
learners, refer to the practices and CORRECTIVE PRINCIPLES in Part I. As with
any set of teaching ideas, select and modify the CORRECTION strategies to meet
the learning needs of individual students.

11. ACQUIRING ORAL LANGUAGE

DETECTION This may be a special skill need of students who:

- Display a limited speaking vocabulary
- Talk in phrases and short sentences
- Use few descriptive words
- Exhibit problems understanding what they hear (SN 3)
- Have obvious difficulty conversing with others (SN 15)

Description. The continued acquisition and expansion of oral language is necessary to student development of sufficient language skills for clear oral and written communication. Several skills are associated with language development, including careful listening, thinking, vocabulary knowledge, accurate articulation, and concentration. Factors such as interest, courtesy, and confidence also contribute to success in oral language. An overall purpose of instruction in oral language development is primarily one of guiding, modeling, and providing opportunities for using language.

Causation. Poorly developed oral language skills are often the result of a lack of language-building experiences at home and school. Young children need language-enriching opportunities through direct experiences and interaction with adults and other children. Using complete sentences at home and experiencing a variety of positive oral language responses to questions make language acquisition easier. Certain auditory acuity and processing difficulties can also cause students to have delayed language development. Students with possible hearing problems should be referred to a specialist the moment a hearing loss is suspected. In addition to specific auditory deficits, the groups of special learners who may exhibit difficulty acquiring and expanding oral language include the language disabled, language different, learning disabled, mentally retarded, and speech disordered.

Implications. Oral language serves as the basis upon which other communications skills are built. A strong oral language background helps students to speak with confidence. Oral language also provides a background of experiences and vocabulary with which to understand reading and to develop writing skills. In a sense, oral language is the fuel by which other language arts are propelled.

CORRECTION Modify these strategies to meet students' learning needs.

1. *Our Talk.* To routinely model embellished language as well as teach concepts, use My Talk to describe and explain your actions as you move about the classroom (e.g., "I am writing on the board the letter *b*"). Use Your Talk to put the words to students' actions (e.g., "Good; you are drawing a circle around the letter *b*").
2. *Mystery Bag.* Place an unnamed object in a bag or small cloth sack. Have students take turns feeling the object and describing how it feels. Of course, they can guess what the object is, but the primary purpose is to help them share the words to describe what they feel.
3. *Word Worries.* Have students take turns briefly telling about anything that worries them. Participation should be on a volunteer basis. Word Wonders or Wishes can also be used. For students who have difficulty getting started, use a few appropriate pictures as the stimuli for discussion.
4. *If's.* Idea starters can be used to lead into describing thoughts. Stimulate talk by having students finish such ideas as: "If I had time," "If I were older," "If I had a car," or "If I were taller."
5. *Picture Cues.* Collect interesting pictures from magazines, books, or posters of many types. Use the pictures to stimulate students to talk by using such questions as: "What do you see in the picture?" "How would you feel if you were in this picture?" or "What does this remind you of?"
6. *My Friend Says.* When working with young children, have them bring in a favorite puppet, doll, or animal. Encourage them to share what their toy friend is thinking. Shy students in particular like this type of activity. Later have peers work together and speak for their toy friends.
7. *Story Lines.* Use picture stories that have no words. Describe the first few pictures and begin telling the story. Then ask a student to keep the story going by "telling" the next picture. Have another student tell about the next picture and so on. Once students become proficient with this format, omit the pictures and tell 4–5 sentences of a story. Have students take turns adding sentences to your story until a logical ending is reached. Model appropriate language by tactfully correcting or expanding students' statements. For example, if a student said, "He go fast," you would say, "Good, Jerry. He ran down the street."
8. *What Am I?* After students have learned to recognize their names and the names of most of their classmates, try What Am I? The object is to whisper the name of an object or event and have the student try to describe what it is without telling the name. Other students should try to guess the object. For example, "I am blue and high up in the air. What am I?"
9. *Extra Practice.* • Send topics home for students to discuss with family members. • Pair students with a younger student to talk about a hobby or special interest. • Set aside "talk time" for students to talk quietly about a choice of 2–3 topics. • Mount pictures of topics that students suggest for "talk time" each day. • Adapt ideas from Special Need 31.

12. RETRIEVING ORAL LANGUAGE

DETECTION This may be a special skill need of students who:

- Seem to search for words to express their thoughts
- Appear confused trying to express thoughts orally
- Are unable to freely express ideas orally
- Use incomplete sentences and phrases in oral communications
- Hesitate to speak
- Exhibit a limited speaking vocabulary (SN 11)

Description. As a part of their language development, students are usually expected to learn to express themselves orally. Oral language development provides the basis for written language production and also serves as the primary means of human communication. Skills involving asking and answering questions, participating in conversations and discussions, and using oral descriptions, explanations, and elaboration are a part of the language development and expression process. Skilled oral communication requires not only that students recognize and understand the words and phrases that label their ideas but also that they are able to retrieve from memory the particular words to orally express their ideas.

Causation. There are two major causes of students' inability to find the exact words to express their ideas: 1) Either their vocabulary is so restricted that they do not have command of enough or the proper words, or 2) they know and understand the words, realize that they know them, but for the moment are unable to retrieve them from memory to use for oral expression. The first cause was discussed as Special Need 11; the second cause is generally the result of either insufficient experience with the terms for facile expression or faulty processing that inhibits or blocks the recall of the words to express the message. Regardless of cause, not only oral expression but also written expression performances suffer. Language- and learning-disabled students in particular may evidence this special need. Some culturally and language-different or hearing-impaired students may also have similar problems.

Implications. In addition to the interruption of speech while searching for words, students who have difficulty retrieving language may also demonstrate narrow vocabularies, use overly simplistic sentence structure, make grammatical errors in oral and written expression, and generally perform below age peers and teacher expectations when listening, reading, and writing. Correction must include extensive vocabulary enrichment, teacher modeling, and the integration of all the language arts, each to reinforce the other. For students who experience much difficulty, seek the services of a licensed speech/language pathologist; seek advice for those whose problems are mild.

CORRECTION Modify these strategies to meet students' learning needs.

1. *Language Retrieval.* To assist students in finding the words to express their ideas, several general procedures are suggested:
   a. Integrate instruction in listening, speaking, reading, and writing.
   b. Use visual aids for language activities whenever possible.
   c. Provide numerous concrete examples and experiences with language concepts.
   d. Give an overview of major concepts using key vocabulary before lessons.
   e. Guide students to verbally summarize each lesson.
   f. Model and reinforce appropriate language.
   g. Frequently consult a speech/language pathologist for guidance.
2. *Experience Stories.* The generation of experience stories can serve as an integrated experience of oral language development, vocabulary building, generating written ideas, and reading comprehension. As an aid to formulating language, provide a stimulating experience to give students something to talk about (e.g., a fieldtrip, sharing about a favorite hobby or toy, holiday events). Discuss the experience, and then have students participate in building an oral story about the topic. Write the story on the board or transparency, and have students chorally read it. Then, duplicate copies of the story to use as the content for instruction in reading, spelling, sentence structure, vocabulary, and techniques of embellishment.
3. *Picture Talks.* Provide interesting pictures and assist students in making up stories or telling about what the pictures mean to them. You may want students to bring pictures from home to use for their Picture Talks. Also use the discussion about the pictures as the stimulus for generating experience stories for use in all the language arts, as in Activity 2.
4. *Vocabulary Ventures.* Provide daily opportunities for students to extend their speaking vocabularies. Model the use of target words in oral stories and sentences. List the words on posters and illustrate each word with a rebus; leave posters on display for students' reference.
5. *Word Resources.* Instruct students in the use of picture dictionaries or the standard dictionary and thesaurus. Teach them to turn to these resources when they have difficulty retrieving words.
6. *Idea Make-Ups.* Following a content-area lesson, give students 3–4 meaningful words or phrases. Have them take turns using the words to make up a story or event after you model the process. The ideas should relate to the topic from which they are taken. Later describe events using several sentences; have students suggest 1–2 words to describe what happened.
7. *Extra Practice.* • Ask students to watch for interesting pictures in magazines and newspapers for use in their Picture Talks. • Have students make flashcards to practice troublesome words. • Adapt ideas from Special Needs 11 and 13.

13. USING ORAL COMMUNICATION SKILLS

DETECTION This may be a special skill need of students who:

- Use phrases and few complete sentences when talking
- Do not use colorful or descriptive language
- Lack poise and confidence while talking
- Rarely volunteer oral responses
- Have trouble using expression or body language when talking
- Often mumble or speak in a whisper
- Exhibit weak listening skills (SN 1–10)

Description. Once students have learned to generate oral language, some have a tendency to talk in an unrelated, unorganized fashion. Many students have a problem listening to others and relating their remarks to the topic. Communicating orally requires students to listen, maintain eye contact, and understand when it is time to talk or listen. Students also need to learn to use voice and body language cues to help communicate feelings and to recognize feelings when others are talking. Using proper expression or intonation can carry as much of the message during oral communication as the words themselves.

Causation. A limited oral language background, lack of practice, little positive encouragement, and underdeveloped listening skills can cause students to have difficulty communicating. If students are unable to listen to others, it may be because of generally weak listening skills. Some students are very shy or insecure about speaking orally for fear of ridicule or rejection of their ideas. Students with articulation or fluency problems or hearing deficits may also be reluctant to speak up. Other special groups of students who may need corrective instruction are the language different, language disabled, behavior disordered, and mentally retarded.

Implications. The proper use of oral communication is a transition stage between generating language and using oral language for a variety of purposes. These are learned behaviors that can usually be corrected through a gradual process of acceptance, patient guidance, and nonthreatening training experiences. Corrective strategies are general ones that can be used to improve conversation from scattered, self-interest use into a sharing expression and receiving of ideas. This means that students must combine listening and speaking to communicate. When weak listening skills are involved, strategies suggested for Special Needs 1–10 should be considered.

CORRECTION Modify these strategies to meet students' learning needs.

1. *See and Say.* This is a variation of the time-honored Show and Tell activity. Students take turns bringing a special object that has been approved by you to share in class. The object is first shown, but not "told." Other students take turns predicting or sharing only one fact they know about the object. After 2–3 minutes of shared conversation, the student holding the object or picture tells what has not already been discussed about the favorite toy, book, or other item.

2. *Freeze.* Give students a topic. Have the first student begin talking about the topic. At some point, usually after 1–2 minutes, say "Freeze." The first talker is to stop in midsentence and the next student is to begin talking where the first student left off. The idea is to continue the speaker's thought. After 1–2 minutes, say "Freeze" again. After several students have had a turn, begin the process again, this time permitting students to select the topic of interest.

3. *Impromptu Conversations.* Make a conscious effort to stop and have informal conversations with students every day. If possible, students should do at least 50% of the talking. You may need to use more questions to elicit responses at first but allow plenty of wait time (5–7 seconds) between your comments and students' responses. Free time, recess, or just before or after school are great times to practice Impromptu Conversations.

4. *Group Talks.* Use small groups of 3–4 students to encourage practice communicating with others. Close supervision will be needed to see that students learn to listen to others, stay on topic, and let every student have a chance to talk. Careful grouping of students will help; for instance, put all the talkers in the same group so that less vocal students will have an easier entry into the conversation and the more communicative students will benefit from having to wait their turn by competing with other verbal students. At first, give students the topic to discuss; later, have them suggest the topic. Pair students who have difficulty; designate one as the speaker and the other as listener until signaled to swap roles.

5. *Student Messengers.* Whenever possible, give less talkative students the opportunity to go to another class, the office, or the school store on an errand. To begin, it may be necessary to give students oral information and send a note along. In the note, restate the information needed and request that your student be encouraged to state the purpose of the trip. Before actually leaving the room students should practice with a friend.

6. *Extra Practice.* • Use a mystery box with a peephole; have students look in and then describe what they see using a tape recorder or by talking with a classmate. • Have 2 students use puppets to carry on a conversation. • Ask students to record a favorite joke or riddle on tape; monitor for appropriateness and then place tapes in a center for classmates.

14. ANSWERING AND ASKING QUESTIONS

DETECTION This may be a special skill need of students who:

- Hesitate to answer questions
- Appear unsure or anxious responding to oral questions
- Rarely ask questions
- Are easily confused by oral questions
- Have trouble stating questions to others
- Do not make effective use of oral communication skills (SN 13)

Description. The ability to answer and ask questions involves many other language arts skills. Because of the close relationship between language processes and questioning strategies, questioning should be dealt with as a part of other studies and not always taught as a separate area. By including questioning as a part of instruction in oral language, listening, and reading development, the utility and transferability of questioning can be optimized. Asking and answering questions can be directly related to both academic studies and daily situations.

Causation. Teachers sometimes assume that students do not answer questions because they do not know the answers. While this often may be true, there are those students who choose not to respond for other reasons. Some teachers continually seek only the correct response and move on. Others ask questions and immediately begin to answer their own questions. Students can be confused by not understanding a question. A final block to student responses involves teacher responses to correct answers. At times, correct responses receive little more than a nod from the teacher, whereas incorrect answers receive too much negative attention. While a lack of study or student background is often responsible for poor responses to questions, inappropriate teacher behaviors can also cause poor responses as well as reluctance to ask questions. Special groups of students who may evidence special needs in this area are the language different, teacher disabled, behavior disordered, hearing impaired, language disabled, learning disabled, and speech disordered.

Implications. The ability to answer and ask questions is seen by some as an indication of preparation and interest. Too few students are taught to ask questions or even recognize that different types of questions can be used. Performance on tests and discussion skills, key activities for grading and evaluating students' knowledge in all subject areas, are affected by student abilities to answer and ask questions. Therefore, instruction and practice in both skills are necessary for all levels of ability and using all subjects as content.

CORRECTION Modify these strategies to meet students' learning needs.

1. *Multiple Responses.* When questioning students, seek more than a single response. When a correct response is received, continue to seek answers; then go back and ask students to help you decide which answer(s) seems most appropriate. Try holding up a finger for each response received as visible recognition of student responses. As a motivator, give 2–3 seconds of eye contact to students who respond to questions.
2. *Question Starters.* Give students the beginnings of questions for them to finish. These can be used as a part of a reading lesson or as a part of any question portion of a lesson.
3. *Question Cues.* When students are unable to respond to a question, use cues that tap into their schema. It is helpful to provide relevant cues that will help students figure out their own answers. For example: "Can anyone tell us how they think Jo Jo felt after the rain? (No response) His bike was washed away. Look at his face in the picture. How does he feel?" By providing them with cues, students will sometimes be able to figure out their own answers and thereby increase their answering and asking skills.
4. *Pinpoint Questions.* When using either literal or inferential questions, tell students to look at a particular paragraph or sentence. Then say, "Look at this sentence (or paragraph) and decide if the team was really a loser." Talk through a few questions to demonstrate how you would figure out the answer. Be sure to ask students how they "think" their answers. Their thoughts will be helpful ideas for those who could not answer.
5. *Question Box.* Provide a Question Box in the room. Sometimes students ask good questions but the questions are unrelated to the current topic of study. When this happens, have them write the question and drop the question in the box. Two or three times a week, open the box and read the questions orally. Provide answers to some questions; for others, have students help to find the answers by asking "Where can we find out about this?"
6. *Question Switches.* To encourage question asking, give students answers and have them make up questions to fit the answers. This can be played as a game using the format of the popular TV show "Jeopardy." This format is also an excellent review for content tests.
7. *Teacher Quiz.* The day before a test, have students take turns asking questions about the subject. They can use notes, textbooks, or other sources to generate questions. Small groups can be formed to make up 3–5 questions each. Then, have students take turns quizzing the teacher.
8. *Extra Practice.* • Have students work in small groups and question each other about reading or content they are studying. • Have teams of students read texts and, on their own, construct study questions for other students to answer. • Model the technique first, then encourage students to take turns reading topic sentences and turning them into questions.

15. PRESENTING AND DISCUSSING

DETECTION This may be a special skill need of students who:

- Have problems speaking in front of others
- Frequently stray off the topic
- Need constant encouragement during oral discussions
- Show signs of anxiety during oral presentations (SN 19)
- Have difficulty organizing written information (SN 41)

Description.   Presenting and discussing are a part of many types of lessons in most subject areas. Learning to participate in oral discussions involves several related language abilities. The components of a good discussion include active listening, questioning, and responding in a more formalized manner than would be expected during a conversation. Discussions require more attention to a specified topic than do general conversations. Presentations require practice and preparation. Presentations are usually more organized than discussions and may include the use of notes and visual aids.

Causation.   A lack of positive, guided practice often causes students to dread presentations. By requiring students to use skills they have never mastered or by subjecting students to possible embarrassment because they lack proper skills and experiences, teachers can add to their fears of presenting. Forcing participation is usually not successful, particularly on a long-term basis. Difficulties discussing and presenting may result from inadequate peer relations, shyness or lack of self-confidence, lack of knowledge about the topic, limited language skills, speech problems, or hearing impairments. Other groups of special students who may tend to experience difficulty include the language different, behavior disordered, and mentally retarded.

Implications.   Presenting a project, book report, or short paper requires students to integrate several language arts skills. Unless some degree of mastery has been attained in speaking, reading, and writing, students may only be able to complete a portion of a presentation. The development of presentations may require teacher guidance, suggestions, and verification. Selecting a topic, locating information, taking notes, writing the text, planning for visuals, and preparing a work copy represent distinct tasks that must be completed before a presentation is made. Mapping and discussions can be used throughout the preparation process to help clarify ideas and decide what to include. Aside from reporting, presentations can be of a more specific nature, such as panel discussions, poetry readings, choral readings, newscasts, and a variety of individually presented plays or musical efforts. Corrective strategies are designed to encourage and acquaint students with components of both good discussions and presentations.

CORRECTION Modify these strategies to meet students' learning needs.

1. *Partner Reports.* For some students, presenting in front of others is a traumatic event. In such cases, pair students and help them divide the preparation and presentation evenly between each pair of presenters. Have students practice until comfortable in front of a mirror and then present to a small group. Permit students to remain seated to present to classmates.

2. *Hot Topics.* When students are beginning to learn about discussing and presenting, suggest hot topics of high interest to motivate both the presenter and the listeners. Fashion, sports, music, famous people, or school projects involving class members can often hold students' interest. Have students select their topic from 3–4 possible choices suggested by the class. If several topics seem inappropriate, narrow the list to include 2 from which they may choose. By beginning with high-interest topics, the following general guidelines can be taught and applied in a meaningful manner:

    a. Guide students to select topics for which 2–4 sources of information are clearly available.

    b. Set limits as to approximate length and format to be used.

    c. Clarify 4 simple parts of a presentation: locating information, taking notes, writing the major points, and practicing the presentation in front of a small group or mirror.

3. *Presentation Maps.* After students locate their information, help them construct semantic maps (see Chapter 1) to organize the development of the presentation. Instead of notes, these maps can also be used to guide the oral delivery and prompt the student to stay on topic.

4. *Banana Panel.* Appoint students to serve on special panels to discuss 2–3 sides of an issue in history, science, or school events. Because a banana has more than 2 sides, the concept of special Banana Panels can be used to help students develop ideas to support more than a single solution or plan of action. Have students present several sides of an issue and then have the class members decide how they stand by voting.

5. *What Do You Think?* For reluctant speakers, it is sometimes necessary to structure discussion with questions. Before asking for comments, provide 3–10 descriptive words on the board that may be helpful to students as they struggle to find the right words to describe or respond to such questions as: What do you think about the character's actions? Do you think our hero was right in what she did? Why? What do you think about having a different ending to the story? Can you think of one?

6. *Extra Practice.* • Ask different students to sit next to you and serve as a co-discussion leader during lessons or in your absence for brief periods of time. • Have students take pictures of peers during presentations to post on a Speakers Spotlight Board; these serve as visual reminders of the oral presentations. • Adapt strategies from Special Needs 19 and 41.

16. USING SOCIAL AMENITIES

DETECTION This may be a special skill need of students who:

- Do not display general courtesy toward others
- Interrupt others frequently
- Have difficulty waiting their turn to talk
- Respond inappropriately to social greetings
- Cannot make introductions
- Rarely say "please," "thank you," or "excuse me"
- Use inappropriate telephone manners
- Seldom offer apologies or compliments

Description. The proper use of social amenities is an outward sign of social maturity. As a part of students' overall development of appropriate oral expression, manners include those types of behaviors that are generally considered to be both appropriate and timely for the purpose of recognizing or acknowledging other individuals, their actions, or their personal reactions. Social amenities include greetings, requests, acknowledgments, introductions, and proper actions for specific situations, such as telephone courtesy. Verbal manners are an outward sign of respect, concern for others, and proper training.

Causation. Like so many other areas of oral expression, the incorrect use or lack of social amenities can be directly related to the prior use and training students receive at home and during early years in school. Those who miss incidental learning, such as slow learners and mentally retarded or hearing-impaired students, may evidence this need, despite having had appropriate and consistent models. Because some learning-disabled youngsters do not accurately interpret nonverbal and social situations, they may fail to consistently observe social conventions. The customs and language patterns of the school culture are also difficult for some culturally or language-different students.

Implications. Students who do not observe the accepted social customs risk being viewed as less capable or impolite and may face social rejection. In addition to the personal benefits of knowing what to say or how and when to respond to others' actions, command of the amenities makes students feel more at ease with peers and adults. Mastery of these skills facilitates growth in language skills and in many types of social interactions.

CORRECTION Modify these strategies to meet students' learning needs.

1. *The Big 2.* "Thank you" and "please" are 2 responses that are generally considered to be a logical starting point. Encourage their use by modeling both with emphasis and noting the times when each is appropriate. Conduct roleplaying sessions using partners in situations requiring "please" or "thank you," and then change partners. Give another situation and ask students to demonstrate an appropriate response. Reinforce the proper use of the terms throughout the school day.

2. *Introductions, Please.* Provide several demonstrations of how to introduce yourself. Begin with the full name and some personal, identifying information. Group students in pairs, and have them practice introducing themselves; then have them switch partners. Follow a similar procedure for introducing friends, strangers, family members, and groups of people. Model the process by playing the part of the introducer and then the introduced; coach the students as needed.

3. *Polite Exchanges.* Giving and receiving compliments requires students to understand the purpose and conditions under which certain comments are exchanged. With a student, demonstrate several different situations, such as receiving a birthday present. Next, coach 2 students to roleplay the same exchange. Alter the scene to include such events as accepting a gift you really do not like or even returning a dirty fork in a restaurant. Each time, have pairs of students imitate the event several times. Later, move on to the use of general compliments and then apologies.

4. *Interpreting Slang.* Many people use slang or sarcasm in their greetings and introductions. Videotape some samples from popular TV programs. Use a variety of popular greetings for students to interpret. Discuss why some are more acceptable than others; then model the appropriate responses and have students follow your model.

5. *Telephone Tips.* Contact your local telephone service company to request a learning kit containing telephones (personal and pay), booklets, or filmstrips. Use the kit to model proper answering, message taking, emergency dialing, handling of crank calls, and information requests. After each demonstration, have students follow your model. As a safety measure, teach the proper response to strangers' questions such as "Who is this? Where do you live? Who is there with you?" Encourage students to act out calls they have received or made. Near the phones, place cards with ideas for calls students can practice.

6. *My Turn.* Conduct roleplaying experiences requiring students to wait for their turn to talk, not interrupt, and listen while others are talking. Designate 1 of a pair of students as the talker and the other as the listener. Have them switch roles on signal. Then group 3–4 students to politely converse about specific topics. Informal meetings can be held to decide what game to play, when to have storytelling time, or what to select as a mascot for the month.

7. *Extra Practice.* • Set up a telephone area where students can practice their conversations. • Have a card bank available for pairs of students to roleplay situations that require responses. • Adapt strategies from Special Needs 13, 14, and 16.

17. USING CREATIVE DRAMATICS

DETECTION This may be a special skill need of students who:

- Appear inhibited participating in creative experiences
- Are self-conscious about creative oral expression
- Reveal a lack of confidence during creative oral expression
- Are unfamiliar with different types of oral expression
- Hesitate to apply oral communication skills (SN 13–16)

Description. Creative dramatic experiences can be among the most interesting and enjoyable activities of the language arts curriculum. Informal drama, pantomime, choral speaking, puppetry, roleplaying, storytelling, and charades are types of creative expression. Students must use their minds, voices, bodies, and creative ideas to communicate in an original way. All students will not be able to participate to the same extent; some students may never become "free spirits." Creative dramatics can be used to encourage the least outgoing students to be less reticent and more able to express ideas and feelings.

Causation. The language arts curriculum is so filled with skill-based components that creative dramatics are usually not given much attention. In practice, some educators feel guilty seeing students so free and having too much fun. Other teachers are uneasy with the seemingly unstructured format of many of the activities. Where there is a heavy emphasis on basic skills, creative dramatics are rarely emphasized beyond the primary grades. Thus, deficits in this area are often the result of very limited in-school experiences. Students who are shy or lack confidence, whatever the cause, may tend to resist creative expression. Those who exhibit speech and language problems or behavior disorders often find these activities threatening. Because gifted students as a group are noted for their creative abilities, they may excel when given appropriate opportunities.

Implications. Spontaneous reactions and expressions of ideas help students to grow and appreciate many art and language forms. The use of creative dramatics has long been a part of the language arts curricula at the primary grade levels, although it is equally valuable at the higher levels. Laughter, free expression, and seeing others in different situations can be helpful for students as they grow and develop behavioral patterns of their own. Creative oral experiences can also serve as a foundation for creative writing of all types. However, a nonjudgmental setting is crucial for creativity to flourish.

CORRECTION Modify these strategies to meet students' learning needs.

1. *Actor's Spotlight.* Roleplaying can be used as an informal means of having students act out situations and events. Following a social studies or reading lesson, have students work together as you guide them to decide how to act out simple stories and events. Take pictures and post them with the names of actors and a caption explaining the presentation.

2. *Actions That Speak.* Pantomime is an appropriate form of nonverbal creative dramatics for those students who are not comfortable speaking in front of others. Select an event from a lesson and guide students to tell the story without talking, using a few basic props. Then have more expressive peers repeat the actions but add the dialogue. Eventually, the pantomimers may be willing to perform both actions and dialogue. You should participate in the first few experiences to both model and show your willingness to perform.

3. *Gesture Plays.* Gesture plays or charades are similar to pantomime except that playing charades involves the audience in guessing what story, title, movie, song, or play is being acted out without words. Begin by having 1–2 students act out a familiar story. If students have trouble guessing, list 3 possible titles, and have them decide which one fits the gesture play they are seeing. Impromptu gesture plays can be presented in 30–60-second intervals if you say to a student "The story is about a happy duck; how would a happy duck walk?" or "This story was about electricity; how do you think you would act if you were a lamp and someone turned you on?" As in Activity 2, have the student who guesses correctly repeat the actions, adding appropriate dialogue.

4. *Puppet Pals.* Puppet shows can serve as a roleplaying experience to retell a story or event, share a special event, and reinforce information in many subject areas. Each student should be given the opportunity to make a puppet (from socks, bags, fans, drawn by hand, etc.), and then have it available for use once or twice a week. Some puppetry guidelines are:
    a. Use only 2–3 puppets in a show.
    b. Have students practice their dialogue without the puppets until they are able to read or talk with expression.
    c. For those who need it, tape the dialogue to play during the show.
    d. Have students practice manipulating a puppet while you talk or play a tape of the dialogue for each scene.
    e. Provide a special stage for the show; use a table with a blanket over it to hide the puppeteers (particularly the shy or reluctant ones).
    f. Include some students as prompters, sound-effect engineers, and discussants after the play.

5. *Extra Practice.* • Have students work in teams to create 3–5-minute puppet shows to interest others in a new book. • Have students read along as they listen to tapes of stories or poems and then supply the sound effects.• Have students dramatize a story to present to younger students.

18. ATTENDING TO LINGUISTIC DIFFERENCES

DETECTION This may be a special skill need of students who:

- Use a dialect that differs from that of the majority culture
- Have problems using Standard English when speaking
- Often appear confused by idioms and figurative language
- Experience difficulty understanding Standard English (SN 18)

Description. No dialect should be judged superior or inferior to another. Some students use what is often called *nonstandard English*; a better descriptor would be *dialectically different*. Everyone has a unique dialect that includes the habitual patterns of sounds, expressions, intonation, accent, fluency, grammar, and usage. These speech patterns were established long before students entered school, and they continue to be reinforced by those of family, friends, and classmates. The importance of a different dialect is not so much how it differs from that of the majority culture but how it interferes with students' understanding the concepts and skills that are typically taught in school using Standard English.

Causation. In the case of students who are linguistically different, the cause is often clear. The dialect of the home differs from Standard American English; differences range from minor to major, as in families who are bilingual or in which no English is spoken. Because initial language development occurs in the home, these language patterns tend to persist, particularly if the dialect is also spoken by close friends. The student and teacher populations of some entire schools are comprised of a subculture that speaks a particular dialect, thereby reinforcing the particular language patterns. Unfortunately for these students, most of the textbooks they will encounter are written in Standard American English.

Implications. It is a mistake to attempt to change students' dialects. Through teacher modeling and use of expansion or alternative choices, students are exposed to standard spoken English. To expect near perfect speech and oral reading is both unrealistic and unnecessary. More pertinent to instruction are the cultural differences that accompany linguistic differences. The cultural differences often indicate an experiential background that differs from the experiences assumed by the curriculum. The language of native American, Mexican-American, or black-American students reflects the values of their family and ethnic group and also affects learning styles and motivation. These cultural factors directly affect how well linguistically different learners perform in school and determine the appropriateness of the learning experiences they encounter.

CORRECTION Modify these strategies to meet students' learning needs.

1. *Cultural Differences.* Consider these guidelines as you implement a language program:
   a. Limit competitive aspects of games and responses; focus on co-operative efforts, fostering group support and group unity.
   b. Involve students of different ethnic backgrounds in leadership roles.
   c. Use interactive lessons that involve frequent use of oral language.
   d. Use supervised small-group participation instead of independent work for all new assignments to permit modeling and co-operation among students.
   e. Provide frequent and continuous oral and aural involvement to help students gain the meaning base they will need for reading and writing.
   f. Avoid using timed responses or speed tests until students feel confident
   g. Involve parents and family in activities whenever possible.
2. *Multilingual Bi-Lines.* When developing key concepts, topics, or headline-type ideas, take the opportunity to highlight additional ways to say, "The Great Debate. Juan, How would we say this in Spanish?" or "Bob, can you tell me another word you can think of that means *great* or *important*?" Give students a chance to use their own language during school time. Many students will work harder if they feel that they can contribute yet are not expected to forget about who they are and how they sound. List some the suggestions on the board. Terms like *main man, big deal*, or *bro* are parallel words that help students feel less linguistically isolated. Make terms more personal and meaningful while also broadening vocabulary knowledge.
3. *Elaboration Exchange.* Many linguistically different students come from homes where the oral interactions between family members are seriously restricted. Responses are often given in short, phraselike statements. Elaboration Exchange involves having students tell more, give an example, or show what they mean as they respond. A buddy system or small groups can be used to share ideas and elaborate on answers and topics of interest.
4. *Community Council.* Have successful linguistically different people from the community visit your class. Ask them to discuss their jobs and the importance of school. Relate the visits to current topics of study.
5. *Extra Practice.* • For discussion and language building, have students bring in their own pictures, music, or special items relating to their culture. • Provide reading material that represents a variety of ethnic backgrounds.

19. REDUCING SPEECH ANXIETY

DETECTION This may be a special skill need of students who:

- Are reluctant to talk in front of others
- Speak in a soft or hesitant voice
- Speak better to individuals and in small groups
- Would rather write than reply orally
- Seldom volunteer during discussions
- Exhibit specific speech problems (SN 21–23)

Description.   Many of us experience anxiety about speaking at one time or another. Typically, stage fright or nervousness is associated with talking in front of a strange group. Speech anxiety can occur any time students have to talk with others, even to only one peer. Nervous mannerisms, articulation difficulties, or panic can be observed when such students talk to a person in authority, a stranger, or a member of the opposite sex. Telephone conversations can also be traumatic. Speech anxiety is directly related to past experiences involving oral expression, the speaker's level of confidence, the expected response of the listener, and the amount of guided practice students have had. Speech anxiety can also cause students to talk excessively or to offer inappropriate comments.

Causation.   Past experience, self-concept, overall mastery of oral language, and personal characteristics all affect levels of anxiety about speaking. The uneasiness may be generalized or associated primarily with a specific circumstance or person. Positive classroom experiences can provide students with coping behaviors as well as confidence in conversational, small-group, and informal situations. Speaking anxiety involving low self-concept may also require the intervention of a counselor. Students who often appear self-conscious and anxious about speaking in front of others are those with speech and language disorders.

Implications.   Everyone does not need to become a toastmaster. However, adequate mastery of oral communications is necessary for students to participate in learning and in social and vocational experiences, both in and out of school. Unless students feel comfortable talking, their tendency will be to retreat or rebel through actions that are counterproductive to academic achievement and positive social growth. Progress toward decreasing anxiety can be made by beginning intervention using a nonthreatening situation and gradually building toward more difficult situations. Students' speech habits reflect in part personality roles they have developed. Knowledge of when and when not to speak, recognition and use of social greetings and spoken etiquette, and conversational manners are learned skills that give students more confidence.

CORRECTION Modify these strategies to meet students' learning needs.

1. *Nonjudgmental Reactions.* One of the most important teacher behaviors for reducing speech anxiety is the use of nonjudgmental or positive responses to student comments. We frequently ask for questions, remarks, and opinions and then proceed to enforce our own views or the right response on students. Anticipation of listener response, positive or negative, can cause a great deal of anxiety. Teachers should set a positive, supportive model of how to react to oral comments.

2. *Multiple-Response II.* When discussing a topic, new vocabulary, or questioning, encourage multiple responses by not accepting just 1 answer and then moving to the next question or topic. Seek a response, acknowledge it with eye contact, and then request additional comments. After obtaining 2–4 possible answers or opinions, guide students toward the most appropriate response. Some teachers like to hold up a finger as a counter to recognize each response. This procedure allows students to see that what they say counts. The purpose of asking questions involves more than seeking answers. It is most effective when it involves interactive learning and discussion.

3. *Soap Box.* Allow time each day for students to take 2–3 minutes and tell about such things as their favorite music, food, place to go, time of year, animal, dreams, pets, or other items of interest. Provide a sign-up sheet and allow time for 2–4 speakers a day. Anxious speakers may feel more comfortable if they use a visual aid as a prop (and for security).

4. *Bothersome Bloopers.* Designate a portion of a bulletin board for posting bloopers from radio and television broadcasts. These also can be found in books, written on cards, and then posted. If students hear a blooper or see one in print, use their bloopers also. It is important to also encourage students to use the errors you make. Students can benefit from knowing that even professionals make mistakes.

5. *Relaxation Ritual.* Teach students a few simple behaviors that may reduce anxiety before speaking. For example, taking a few deep breaths and thinking about something relaxing or peaceful can help.

6. *Positive Repetition.* Ask students to use self-talk or silent thoughts to reassure themselves when anxiety occurs. Use examples of what you might say to yourself to build confidence and reduce anxiety.

7. *Extra Practice.* • Provide a tape recorder in a corner of the room for students to use to make oral notes and expressions of anger or joy when they feel the need. • Pair students with a younger student from another class, and have them explain a story, mathematics operation, or other information during a 5-minute lesson. • Make grouping decisions so that somewhat reluctant speakers are grouped together and the more talkative students are together; this enables the less talkative students to have a chance to participate. • Adapt strategies from Special Needs 21 and 23.

20. USING DIFFERENT FORMS OF PRESENTATION

DETECTION This may be a special skill need of students who:

- Tend to cling to one presentation format
- Prefer to read aloud from a written report
- Appear uneasy about speaking in front of others
- Prefer to present as a group rather than individually
- Display nervous behaviors when speaking to others (SN 19)

Description. Satisfactory use of different forms of presentation is not considered to be a prerequisite skill when compared to other types of special needs in speech. Presentation skills can serve as an appropriate extension for those students who have mastered more basic speaking skills or for those students whose personalities tend to lead them toward more extroverted behaviors. Knowing several different formats and methods of reporting can help students gain confidence, appreciate speaking skills, and enjoy being able to participate in socially oriented experiences.

Causation. Good presentations require planning, practice, confidence, and general speaking experience. Problems students experience preparing or presenting a speech often relate to one of these areas. Being unprepared, nervous, and unconfident can also cause students to have problems making presentations. Students who are self-conscious about a speech or language disability may be reluctant to speak before others, even if they have mastered the different formats of presentation.

Implications. Even for adults, speaking or presenting in front of others carries its own type of anxiety or pressure. A major point involved in teaching presentation skills is to assist students in communicating more easily and with clarity. The teacher's role is largely one of creating and modeling opportunities for students to participate in varied types of presentations and communication formats. Information provided in Chapter 7 may also be useful in developing a strong skill base upon which presentation experience can be built.

CORRECTION Modify these strategies to meet students' learning needs.

1. *Book Blurbs.* Book Blurbs is a technique in which students select 3 interesting events, ideas, or circumstances from a book and then develop a headline and 2 sentences describing each of the 3 points of interest. These statements can then be presented in minireports to the class or in small groups.

2. *Divergent Delivery.* Using a topic of high interest, help students develop stories, problems, or other items of special concern. Have the same information presented using more than a single method of presentation. For example, to help explain the workings of the transportation system, ask a student to share information in the form of a news report; have other students present the information as a short play; request that another group hold a panel discussion. To begin, give all students or groups the same background information and assist them in developing their delivery formats.

3. *Focused Readings.* On a volunteer basis, encourage students to read to the class from a favorite story or book for a 2–3 minute interval. Help students select an interesting portion of the material, and allow plenty of time for students to preread their material before reading orally to the class. Plan with the students alternate means of presenting the selection; then assist in the implementation of the chosen format.

4. *Personalized Interviews.* Ask 1–2 students to interview someone in the school. Have a practice interview during which students can rehearse their questioning and notetaking techniques. After the interview, have students share their findings with other class members through a panel discussion or report. Gradually expand the interview process by suggesting that persons outside the school be interviewed.

5. *Hear Ye, Hear Ye.* Appoint students to make daily announcements about events, assignments, and other important information. Making announcements requires attention to details and precise explanation. Model the process of developing an announcement. Begin by isolating the reason for the announcement, considering the content required, and deciding upon the most appropriate delivery format.

6. *Visual Variations.* Help students develop graphics to use with presentations. Props, transparencies, slides, charts, and computer graphics are representative of the types of visuals students can develop to enhance the delivery of oral presentations.

7. *Video Samples.* Use a videotape recorder and tape portions of student presentations. Tapes can be valuable sources of information. However, remember that in using the videotapes, the potential for embarrassment is great, and student anxiety about being taped may also be high. Have students rehearse in front of a mirror before taping; then you and the target student should preview tapes before showing them, selecting only sample portions that illustrate constructive points.

8. *Extra Practice.* • Encourage students to practice presentations in front of family at home. • Have students practice mini–choral reading in pairs. • Have a tape recorder available for students to use to record their reports, use for interviews, and then play back for editing. • Provide videotapes of good presentations from TV or other classes; have students watch for positive and negative aspects. • Adapt ideas from Special Needs 15 and 19.

21. ARTICULATING CORRECTLY

DETECTION This may be a special skill need of students who:

- Substitute phonemes while talking
- Distort specific phonemes when speaking
- Omit phonemes when talking
- Insert phonemes unnecessarily when speaking
- Have difficulty discriminating sounds
- Appear anxious when speaking (SN 19)

Description. Articulation refers to how clearly students are able to pronounce phonemes or sounds. Technically, speech sounds include phonetic and phonological levels. Proper articulation enables one to speak precisely and thereby enable listeners to distinguish one word from another. Anytime you find yourself listening to how a student produces words instead of listening to the words themselves, you need to refer that student to the proper authority. Articulation disorders can be diagnosed and dealt with most effectively by licensed speech pathologists. However, when coordinated by a speech specialist, limited classroom interventions are appropriate for the less serious articulation disorders.

Causation. Articulation disorders can be caused by neurological deficits, physical abnormalities, or possibly functional disorders. Functional difficulties include those for which a cause cannot accurately be determined but are considered to be learned, developmental, and nonorganic in nature. Two additional causes of articulation difficulties include poor speech sound discrimination and arrested sensory-motor development. Students who are culturally or language different often mispronounce specific sounds. Certain types of more complex articulation difficulties are characteristic of students with cleft palates, cerebral palsy, or hearing impairments. Only a trained speech pathologist or medical specialist can make specific determinations of causation on an individual basis.

Implications. Because treatment of articulation difficulties is very specialized, consult a speech pathologist before beginning intervention. If the DETECTIVE behaviors listed above are noticed but are not evidenced to excess, the strategies suggested in this section may be useful. At times, most children and adults experience some degree of difficulty in articulation or enunciation. Suggestions are very specific and isolated in scope when compared to suggestions for other language arts areas. However, directed practice is the rule, not the exception. Prerequisite abilities include short- and long-term memory, auditory discrimination, following directions, and imitation.

CORRECTION Modify these strategies to meet students' learning needs.

1. *Prerequisites.* Utilize the CORRECTION strategies for Special Needs 1–7 to develop the prerequisite skills for enunciation of target sounds. In addition, consider these general recommendations:
    a. Rely on the speech pathologist to advise the best corrective program for the classroom.
    b. Offer teacher and peer understanding and support.
    c. Focus on the content of the students' speech, not enunciation.
    d. Provide frequent, consistent, but tactful corrective speech feedback.
    e. Model appropriate speech.
    f. Encourage and arrange for social interaction.
    g. Reinforce content of the speech program with the other language arts.
2. *Three-Phase Practice.* The three phases of remediation recommended by the speech pathologist will likely include:
    a. *Awareness*: Inform students of the sound (phoneme) and its correct pronunciation. Help them listen for the sound and discriminate its uniqueness in comparison to other sounds.
    b. *Acquisition*: Provide specific, repeated practice producing the target sound in isolation in different positions of nonsense syllables.
    c. *Automatization*: Continue the Acquisition phase until the student is able to make the sound without having to stop and think about its pronunciation; then provide practice using real words that contain the target sound, first in isolation and then in context.
2. *Follow Me.* Show students a physical means of producing or verifying a target sound. For example, demonstrate a method of making the "f" sound by placing an index finger horizontally just below the lower lip. Then by moving the upper lip slightly forward, blow lightly to make the "f" sound.
3. *Speech Helpers.* Teach the names of the body parts that help in making sounds, such as the voice box, lips, tongue, and teeth. Then explain the role and position of each in making the target sounds. Model and then have students watch in a mirror to compare their performance with yours.
4. *Word Helpers.* If possible, find 1–2 two words students can pronounce correctly using the problem phoneme in any position (initial, final, medial). Teach students to use these Word Helpers as concrete references.
5. *Nonsense to Sense.* Teaching students to produce problem sounds in isolation may be helpful in some cases. Once the single sound is mastered, it is then used in a word or grouping of nonsense syllables. If nonsense syllables are used, a third step should involve using the misarticulated sound in words and then in context. Practice sessions should include repeating the sound in succession numerous times until mastered.
6. *Extra Practice.* • Have students practice in front of a mirror. • Tape students' practice sessions and then critique the tapes with students. • Adapt strategies from Special Needs 2 and 19.

22. USING PROPER VOICE

DETECTION This may be a special skill need of students who:

- Use a weak or whispered voice
- Speak in a loud, almost yelling tone
- Reveal a harsh or rough tone
- Talk in a very shrill or high-pitched voice
- Use a very nasal-sounding voice
- Converse in a monotone voice

Description.   Voice disorders includes problems related to intensity, pitch, and quality. Problems involving intensity can be classified as being too loud, too soft, or weak, ranging from complete nonproduction of sound to highly stressed, whispered sounds. Pitch disorders can be grouped into six to eight categories, but in general, pitch refers to the highness or lowness of the voice. Among the most frequent problems associated with voice difficulties are those related to quality, or the smoothness or resonance of the voice. Excessive nasalness, harshness, or breathiness are associated with voice-quality problems. The classroom teacher's role in the correction of voice problems is often one of following the instructions of a properly credentialed speech pathologist.

Causation.   Voice disorders, less common than articulation difficulties, can result from organic physical problems. Disorders of the voice can also be caused by emotional problems or voice abuse. Young adolescents who abuse their voices by singing, yelling, or smoking are likely to experience voice difficulties. Students who are hearing impaired often have difficulty regulating the intensity, pitch, and quality of speech. Certain physical and medical handicaps are sometimes accompanied by voice disorders.

Implications.   An obvious point in student development that is often associated with voice difficulties is adolescence, or puberty. The numerous physical changes that occur sometimes involve voice pitch, quality, and intensity at the same time, particularly in males. Although often transient in nature, these difficulties may create distress and embarrassment. Proper teacher modeling and a positive communications atmosphere are necessary. Of particular importance is the early recognition of vocal abuse, especially in young children, to prevent permanent physical damage. Students who demonstrate such habits as chronic screaming, screeching, or other forms of voice strain should be immediately referred to a speech pathologist. All voice problems require medical clearance before any corrective program is initiated. Some voice difficulties can only be remedied by surgical procedures with training thereafter coordinated by a physician and a speech pathologist.

CORRECTION Under the supervision of a speech pathologist, try these strategies.

1. *Voice Rules.* When working with students with diagnosed voice problems, several general practices are recommended:
    a. Carefully follow the instructions of the speech pathologist.
    b. Develop a system to signal the student when the voice is being abused.
    c. Develop a system for the student to signal you when the voice tires.
    d. Limit the duration of oral exercises.
    e. Alternate oral and silent lessons to permit vocal rest.
2. *Physical Fitness.* Proper posture, full breathing, and the ability to relax can help students to have better speaking voices. Deep breathing and relaxation before singing, speaking, or oral reading can reduce tension and make speaking less difficult.
3. *Sound Sources.* Some students need help distinguishing between different sounds. Contact a local band instructor for assistance in prerecording 1–2 notes using several different musical instruments. You will also need records or audiotapes of the same instruments being used in a song. If possible, have a music teacher bring in several instruments and participate using the instruments. Then, help students identify which instruments make which sounds. Use such questions as: Which instrument makes the loudest noise? Which of these 2 instruments is played by blowing (play a drum and a flute or horn)? Which sound is lower (play a triangle and a trombone)? Follow a similar procedure with other types of sounds.
4. *Comparative Analysis.* Students should learn how to recognize and discriminate between different voices. This can be learned by listening experiences. Have students listen to audiotapes of student, radio, or television speakers. Have them listen for the person with the highest- or lowest-pitched or weakest voice. Then ask, "Which person does your voice sound the most like?" Other comparisons can be made for singers who are softer or louder while others are sharper, more hoarse, or nasal sounding. Students can benefit from listening and recognizing that different people have different voices.
5. *Radio Controls.* To help students learn to control pitch, have them begin by making a humming sound with their mouth closed or only slightly open. Then ask them to make the sound louder, then louder or higher, then higher. You both will notice a change in the tone. Students will begin to see that they can control the sounds they make. Have students pretend they are going higher and higher in an elevator or airplane, turning up a radio, or so on.
6. *Extra Practice.* • If they have a favorite announcer or speaker, encourage students to practice speaking like him or her. • Have students listen to tapes to compare and describe voices as high/low, loud/soft, harsh/soft; or have them tape their own oral reading, word pronunciation, or oral presentations and then evaluate their voices. • Adapt ideas from Special Needs 1–7.

23. MINIMIZING STUTTERING

DETECTION This may be a special skill need of students who:

- Repeat the first syllable of words
- Often repeat whole words or phrases
- Prolong certain syllables
- Strain to speak but make no sound
- Exaggerate mouth and lip movements
- Display lip tremors or breathe unevenly during speech
- Have a voice that sounds stressed
- Appear anxious when speaking (SN 19)

Description. Stuttering, the most prevalent form of speech disfluency, is characterized by interruptions or blockages of speech, accessory features associated with breathing, stress, exaggerated mouth movements, sometimes physical movements, and often emotional reactions to the stuttering. Miscommunication often results because of the distorted speech and occasionally the blurting out of a different word from the one intended. Many stutterers feel embarrassed, segregated, and frustrated by not being able to express themselves freely. They often seek out persons they hope will be patient and listen. These students know what they want to say but are unable to express the information fluently. Their frustration and embarrassment can lead to emotional complications, particularly if teachers and peers seem to notice or appear uncomfortable.

Causation. More is known about what does *not* cause stuttering than about what *does*. The notion that stuttering is a form of neurosis is no longer prevalent. Serious emotional trauma, while reported to cause occasional disfluencies, cannot account for all cases. There is little evidence that students begin stuttering as an imitative function, such as associating with a stutterer. Parental practices requiring perfection in manners, speech, and daily activities that may produce anxiety have not been shown as a definite cause of stuttering. Inheritance, laterality, and biochemical reactions are also considered to be unlikely causes, although disfluencies do tend to occur more frequently in some families than in others. Since speech production involves fine-motor coordination, nerve connections, and other physical aspects, there is some basis for suspecting that there may be an organic explanation for stuttering.

Implications. The single greatest implication is that stuttering students need to experience extreme patience and acceptance on the part of their teachers and peers. These students should be addressed in a normal voice, not a slower or louder voice. They often feel uncertain about what will come out every time they speak. Teachers can help reduce this stress by being patient and supportive, not nervous or embarrassed. Although stuttering may tend to worsen during moments of stress, when students respond to a script, as in oral reading, stuttering may disappear. The direction and coordination of a speech pathologist are crucial to the success of a corrective program.

CORRECTION Modify these strategies to meet students' learning needs.

1. *Acceptance.* Acceptance and support by teachers and peers are particularly important to the improvement of speech skills. Among the practices that appear to facilitate communication of disfluent speakers are these:
    a. Do focus on the content, not the style of the speaker.
    b. Do look directly at the student when he or she is speaking.
    c. Do tactfully restate words correctly if the message is unclear.
    d. Do not call attention to the stuttering.
    e. Do not attempt to intercede or speak for the student.
    f. Do not tell the student to slow down or start over.
2. *Emotional Communication.* People communicate emotionally through facial expressions, touch, or willingness to listen. The concept of the emotional communication between young child and mother can be applied to include teachers who care and accept students without judgment or embarrassment. See that family and peers do not tease or hurry students.
3. *Therapeutic Play.* Engage the students in play or hobby activities. Building models, assembling mechanical items, conducting experiments, using favorite toys, games, or even computer play can provide a relaxed period during which stutterers can communicate without pressure. The association with the student will also make teachers familiar with the speech problem and help them understand what the student says during regular lessons. Such play can also provide a time for building stronger, personal bonds.
4. *Fluency.* Carefully observe students to identify the oral activities during which their speech is most fluent. For many students, stuttering all but disappears during activities such as choral reading, recitation of poems or other memorized text, and singing. Once the activity is identified, provide ample opportunities for the student to perform as a fluent speaker. Occasionally, the fluency may transfer to other speech by having the student, for example, think about or pretend to sing when reading aloud.
5. *Creative Interactions.* Acting out through informal, creative dramatics or roleplaying can offer students the chance to perform as someone else. During such times, disfluencies may be reduced or less obstructive.
6. *Encourage Self-Talk.* Self-Talk involves students in situations in which they engage in a dialogue with themselves, a favorite animal, pretend audience, or pet. During Self-Talk, disfluencies are sometimes reduced.
7. *Extra Practice.* • Tape familiar stories and have students read along with the tape. • Suggest that students talk along or sing along with the radio.• Have students conduct pretend interviews with a favorite personality.• Encourage students to talk while playing video or computer games.

REFLECTIONS

1. A general overview of speaking skills is presented in the introduction to Part III. To review this section, reread the opening discussion and then formulate questions to ask a licensed speech pathologist.

2. Part III separates oral expression and speech into two different chapters and notes that the two areas are distinct but related. Review the specific skills cited for each chapter to identify the similarities and differences. Which ones have the most in common? The least? How would you organize these Special Needs? Justify your scheme.

3. In the first paragraph of the discussion of each Special Need, the different skills are described. Reread these descriptions to decide why each skill is important to general academic functioning. Next, identify only three that you consider to be the most crucial to the success of students with identified learning problems. Which three do you consider to be the most vital to the progress of nonhandicapped students? Reconcile the differences if any in the skills you selected for each group. Would your selections vary according to the age of the students? Why or why not?

4. The discussion of each Special Need begins with a list of DETECTION behaviors that signal problems in a particular speaking skill. Observe in a speech and language therapy class to watch for these behaviors. Record any additional problem behaviors that you observe and then ask the speech pathologist to add to the list. Next, observe in a special education classroom and follow similar procedures.

5. CORRECTIVE PRINCIPLES for categories of special students are presented in Chapters 2 and 3. Select a real or hypothetical special learner with an identified oral expression need. Use the CORRECTIVE PRINCIPLES as guidelines to select and modify the CORRECTION strategies to meet the probable learning needs of the selected student; then repeat the procedures for a student with an identified speech problem.

6. Speaking is the major means of communication, both in and out of school. Observe in a regular classroom and in a special education class to note the types of speaking activities and to determine the amount of time students are engaged in oral language. Compare and contrast your findings in the two settings and then explain any differences.

7. Many students as well as adults are apprehensive when speaking to an audience of peers. Consider the last time you were the featured speaker. What strategies did you use to make yourself feel comfortable? Review the CORRECTION strategies for Special Need 19, Reducing Speech Anxiety, to identify any techniques that would help you. Then add your suggestions to those listed. How would your needs compare with those of a severe stutterer? A learning-disabled student?

8. Structured speaking opportunities must be integrated throughout the curriculum. Plan two speaking-improvement activities to be incorporated into a reading lesson and a science or social studies lesson for a special learner. Use the diagnostic information available from the school, lesson content that matches the learner's skill needs and interests, and the CORRECTIVE PRINCIPLES to guide the selection and modification of one or more of the CORRECTION strategies listed for presenting and discussing, Special Need 15.

9. Implementation of special lessons often includes adjustments during teaching. Practice with a peer the speaking lessons you designed for the special learner. Then teach those lessons to the special learner, modifying your plans according to the student's needs as you teach.

10. A number of suggestions for teaching speaking skills to a variety of learners are presented in language arts, special education, and speech and language textbooks. Compare and contrast discussions in these sources with the information in Chapters 7 and 8:

Boone, D. R. (1987). *Human communication and its disorders*. Englewood Cliffs, NJ: Prentice-Hall.

Culler, T. (1984). *Articulation disorders: A basic guide to intervention in the schools*. Austin, TX: Pro-Ed.

Hoskisson, K., & Tompkins, G. E. (1987). *Language arts: Content and teaching strategies*. Columbus, OH: Charles E. Merrill.

Lewis, R. B., & Doorlag, D. H. (1987). *Teaching special students in the mainstream* (2nd ed.). Columbus, OH: Charles E. Merrill.

Petty, W. T., Petty, D. C., & Becking, M. F. (1985). *Experiences in language: Tools and techniques for language arts methods* (4th ed.). Boston: Allyn and Bacon.

Polloway, E. A., & Smith, J. E. (1982). *Teaching language skills to exceptional learners*. Denver: Love.

Shames, G. H., & Wiig, E. H. (1986). *Human communication disorders* (2nd ed.). Columbus, OH: Charles E. Merrill.

Wallace, G., Cohen, S. B., & Polloway, E. A. (1987). *Language arts: Teaching exceptional students*. Austin, TX: Pro-Ed.

Wallach, G. P., & Miller, L. (1988). *Language intervention and academic success*. Boston: College-Hill/Little, Brown.

PART IV

SPECIAL READING NEEDS

Reading is often considered to be the single most important skill of academic curricula, both as a subject itself at the lower levels and as the major source of learning in all subjects as students advance through the curriculum. Like listening, reading is a decoding task in which the reader deciphers and then interprets the written message. Developmentally, reading is not a stand-alone basic skill area set apart from the language arts but rather a companion skill that is best mastered in concert with writing and supported by listening and speaking skills.

Because reading is so crucial to academic success, there is a tendency to move too quickly from listening and speaking development directly into the teaching of reading. When reading is viewed as a part of the overall language process, formal reading instruction can be delayed until students have gained a degree of mastery of listening and speaking skills. This does not mean that students should not have books or participate in prereading experiences. Being read to, owning books, and reading signs, posters, and other topical information are a part of reading instruction in the broadest sense. Just as learning to print one's name is a part of learning to write, so is learning to handle, listen to, and talk about the information in books a part of reading instruction.

There are as many different skills groupings for reading as there are reading textbooks and reading programs. In Part IV, the reading skills are categorized as: word recognition, comprehension, and study skills. Chapters 9 through 11 each address topics that are treated as whole, separate chapters in some publications, such as those cited at the end of this section. However, in this book, each of these topics is treated as a recurring theme throughout the discussions of listening, speaking, or writing.

Chapter 9 focuses on word-recognition skills, important tools for reading and comprehension. Four types of word-recognition skills are discussed, beginning with sight vocabulary, the letters and words that occur often in text and that readers must recognize instantly. Phonic analysis, or "sounding out" words to pronounce them, and structural analysis, the use of word parts to decode them, are both pronunciation skills. Once words are pronounced, if they are ones students understand as part of their listening and speaking vocabularies, then word reading occurs. The most powerful of the word-recognition skills is contextual analysis because it offers clues to both pronunciation and meaning.

Comprehension, the essence of reading, is discussed in Chapter 10. Two of the general comprehension patterns, oral and silent reading, represent the primary means through which reading is taught and evaluated. The third global type of reading, reading for pleasure, is the one least often encouraged or taught to most students, and it is seldom if ever presented to students with special needs. Several interrelated facets of the comprehension process are discussed as specific skills for purposes of identifying the strategies that students need to be taught. The understanding of word meanings contributes to both word recognition and overall comprehension. Literal comprehension requires readers to understand and recall text-explicit information, while inferential comprehension involves the understanding of text-implicit information. Critical comprehension entails understanding and then evaluating text.

Study skills enable students to learn independently both in school and in later life. Yet, as discussed in Chapter 11, these are the skills often demanded but seldom taught in school.

DETECTION OF SPECIAL READING NEEDS

Teachers readily recognize students who have difficulty reading because reading is such an integral part of academia. However, identifying the nature and extent of the reading problems is not so easily accomplished. Options for diagnosing reading needs are far more numerous than those for analyzing the other language arts skills; nonetheless, because of the complexity of the reading process, no one measure is clearly best.

Formal Detection

Reading abilities are often tested as part of standardized group-administered achievement tests. Among the reading skills typically measured are sight vocabulary, word comprehension, contextual analysis, and silent comprehension. Because of the nature of the group-testing format, such tests may inadvertently measure reading comprehension when purporting to test content areas like social studies or science. Some special students are unable to demonstrate their knowledge on these tests because of problems tracking the correct bubble to mark on the answer sheet, the pressures of time and the increasingly difficult items, and misinterpretation of questions and directions. As a screening device, scores from these tests may point to the need to analyze a student's reading skills on an individual basis.

Standardized, individually administered tests of reading are frequently a part of the evaluation of students who are suspected of being exceptional. These tests often include measures of sight vocabulary and silent or oral comprehension. The other types of reading skills that are tested vary according to particular tests. Because of the standardized procedures, including timelines, some special students are unable to demonstrate all of their reading abilities. The test formats usually permit careful clinical observations of the student's performance, adding important diagnostic data.

Informal Detection

The most popular informal test format is the informal reading inventory (IRI). This format uses a set of graded passages and questions to determine a general reading comprehension level and sometimes a comprehension profile. Most IRIs include lists of words and procedures for assessing several of the word-recognition skills, particularly sight vocabulary and phonics. Such techniques as having students retell or paraphrase passage content, supply the missing words in passages, or verify sentences are alternative reading assessment formats. Regardless of format, incorrect answers, words, or pronunciations or inaccurate retellings are used as clues to the reading skills that students have not mastered.

Classroom observations of students as they read and discuss their readings can yield considerable diagnostic data. Behaviors that may indicate a particular reading problem are listed at the beginning of the discussion of each special need (DETECTION). Related Special Needs are noted in parentheses. Although these behaviors alone do not verify a skill need, when they are demonstrated consistently and are confirmed by daily oral and written work, you have probably located the logical point at which to begin corrective instruction.

A large majority of all types of special students read below their theoretical capacity or their chronological age level. Even some gifted students are underachieving readers. Like problems in the other language areas, the causes of reading difficulties are varied and range from inadequate mastery of the prerequisite listening and speaking skills to sensory, physical, intellectual, environmental, and experiential differences.

CORRECTION OF SPECIAL READING NEEDS

Difficulties recognizing words slow and interfere with the reading comprehension process. Comprehension problems affect more than just the reader's performance in reading class. Poor readers are typically poor writers and are unduly penalized in most all other curricular areas as well. With proper instruction, some of the word-recognition skills can be improved fairly quickly. In contrast, the effects of corrective comprehension strategies may not be realized for some time. Because study skills must become habits to be effective, they too often appear to respond slowly to correction.

The correction of reading problems requires consistent, focused, and direct intervention built upon listening and speaking skills, leading to writing experiences. Such integration also provides a more multisensory approach to teaching. Experiences related to the reading content must be built or recalled with students prior to reading. Both word-recognition and comprehension skills must be applied in the context of meaningful passages. Correction of study skills should be incorporated into lessons in every subject. Teacher modeling accompanied by directing the students to follow the model is a particularly valuable technique for teaching fluent oral reading, self-questioning while reading, predicting and verifying, various study skills, and the vital thinking strategies for evaluating text.

Care should be taken in selecting materials for skill-specific instruction to insure that the structure of the text fits the specific type of reading experience. For general guidelines to develop and implement strategies to teach identified special learners, consult the CORRECTIVE PRINCIPLES in Part I. As in previous sections, it is important to choose and modify each strategy to meet the specific learning needs of individual students.

24. REMEMBERING LETTERS AND SIGHT WORDS

DETECTION This may be a special skill need of students who:

- Often confuse letters
- Are unable to remember certain letters
- Need assistance pronouncing easy words
- Exhibit an inadequate sight vocabulary
- Reveal problems remembering sight words

Description. An inability to recall letters or identify basic sight words can cause students to experience serious problems reading. As many as half or even more of the words appearing in printed material can be classified as sight words. Several popular lists have been developed based upon frequency counts of words appearing in instructional and tradebook materials. It is essential that students develop a large sight-word vocabulary if they are to sustain progress in reading. The burden of having to decode each word individually unduly slows the reading rate, increases the complexity of the task, and causes students to lose comprehension.

Causation. Problems remembering letters can stem from difficulty discriminating letters and shapes or problems involving visual memory. Sight-word recall is sometimes hampered by students' inability to conceptualize words without concrete meaning or structural clues. Many high-frequency words, such as *the, and, for, to,* and *that,* have little concrete meaning and few distinguishing features and are thus difficult for some students to remember. Some learning-disabled and visually impaired students may experience particular difficulty recalling letters and sight words.

Implications. Many experts consider letter mastery as prerequisite for learning to read. It is possible to read without first learning all the letters of the alphabet; some gifted or highly verbal students appear to begin reading without mastery of letters. However, except for a select few students, reading instruction appears to be easier and more effective when students are able to recognize letters. Teaching sight words does not signify the exclusive use of the look-say or whole-word approach. A variety of decoding strategies, including phonic analysis, should parallel specific instruction for developing a sight-word vocabulary. Students who experience particular difficulty mastering phonics may need to rely more heavily on their memory for letters and sight words.

CORRECTION Modify these strategies to meet students' learning needs.

1. *High-Frequency Letters.* Letters used in students' names, their school's name, or other high-interest words should be taught. The incidence of high-frequency letters in familiar words will make mastery easier. This may be accomplished by having students say the letters as they trace them with a felttip marker or underline or circle specific letters.

2. *Look Alikes.* Print letters or words on 3" x 5" index cards. Use the cards in a variety of ways, including flash recognition, flash matching, or a card game matching like letters or words.

3. *Initial or Final Letter Match.* Show students a letter and then 2–3 words. Have them name the word that begins or ends with the target letter.

4. *Image Writing.* Have students say and "image-write" target letters or words. Write each letter or word on the chalkboard, placing above it a key picture such as a dog for *d*, a house for *house*, or a boy for *the* boy. Have students use their index fingers to repeatedly trace the letter or word while saying its name. With each tracing, more chalk is erased, leaving the image of the original markings. When the image is almost invisible, have students close their eyes and try to see the letter or word, and then trace the image with chalk, again saying the letter or word.

5. *Sight-Word Cloze.* Use a modified cloze format and have students either select the correct sight word from 3 choices or fill in an appropriate sight word in the blanks of simple sentences. As each word is correctly selected, have students trace or write it while saying it.

6. *Sight-Word Bingo.* Print 12–20 different sight words in boxes on cards in a manner similar to numbers appearing on a Bingo card. Call out sight words and have students mark their cards. Determine winners according to the ability levels of your students. Use rows of 3 or more or the traditional across, down, and diagonal row completions.

7. *Word Work-Outs.* Form teams and either show a sight word on a card or print a word on the board. Have the first team pronounce the first word; then move to the second team with a different word. If one team misses a word, the other team gets a chance. Students can take turns participating as a total group, as groups of 2–3, or as individual team members.

8. *Extra Practice.* • Use Activity 6, but print letters on the Bingo cards instead of sight words. • Ask students to keep lists of words they see around the house or anywhere out of school that they recognize. • Highlight 2–5 sight words a day as honor words; in addition to pronouncing and teaching these words, have students work in pairs and quiz each other using several days' honor words on cards.

25. USING PHONIC ANALYSIS

DETECTION This may be a special skill need of students who:

- Do not remember the sounds of certain letters
- Are unable to sound out unfamiliar words
- Refuse to try to pronounce unfamiliar words
- Cannot blend sounds into words
- Have difficulty discriminating sounds (SN 1)
- Do not remember much of what they hear (SN 6)

Description. Phonic analysis is one of several important word-recognition skills necessary for decoding words. Phonics involves the relationship between speech and written symbols. The English language is based on a system of letter/sound combinations. The sounds of the consonants are generally much more stable than the sounds of vowels. Phonetic inconsistencies are created by letters having different sounds depending upon their use in varied combinations. Over 300 phonic generalizations could be used to teach students to sound out words. However, 20 or so of these are generally accepted as being useful. Of these 20, the few that are the most reliable appear to be those associated with short and long vowel sounds and the different sounds of *c* and *g*. For phonic analysis to facilitate the pronunciation of words, direct instruction must begin with the high-utility generalizations used in a whole-word context.

Causation. Difficulty applying phonic analysis to the decoding of words may result from students' inability to remember the letter sounds because of visual or auditory problems or boredom with the task. Students who recall the sounds but do not apply them may not have had sufficient opportunities to practice the skills in context or direct instruction in blending the sounds into words. Students who prefer a more visual learning style or who are linguistically different often have problems using phonic analysis. Other sources of possible difficulty include slow learning rates, learning disabilities, hearing impairments, mental retardation, and speech disorders.

Implications. For the past 100 years, debate has raged over the degree, amount, sequence, and approach that should be used when teaching phonics. While most experts agree that training in phonic analysis is necessary, there is little consensus on the duration and approach that work best. Most specialists advise beginning by teaching consonant sounds and then vowel sounds. Others prefer to teach phonics as a less structured process based upon the students' use of written language. Still others disclaim the analytic methods using whole words and instead encourage teaching letters and graphemes in isolation and then following with word-blending experiences. Special learners, in particular, need a systematic approach that stresses the most reliable of the phonetic components. Consonant sounds tend to be the most stable; those in the initial position of words seem most useful and their use reinforces the left-to-right concept. Thus, initial consonants are the most logical starting point for corrective instruction. In fact, pairing the use of context with the initial sounds of words may be enough to decode many words. In addition to the strategies listed below, many of the ideas suggested in remedial and basal reading programs can be adapted to meet individual needs.

CORRECTION Modify these strategies to meet students' learning needs.

1. *Single Consonant Sounds.* With each of these activities, use a key picture to illustrate the target sound, stress its pronunciation, highlight it with a marker, write it on the board, and have students write it as they say it:
    a) Call out a word and have students either select or print the consonant with which the word begins or ends;
    b) Give students a target sound and have them tell or write words using the target initial consonant;
    c) Use a cardboard roll from paper towels as a chimney and ask students to pronounce words with certain beginning consonants and then drop them down the Consonant Chimney if correct;
    d) Give students short phrases with a key word underlined, followed by a partial word in which to fill in the missing consonant; and
    e) Have students suggest different initial consonants for rhyming words (e.g., *ran/_an*) for Consonant Substitution.
2. *Word Families.* Use word families or rhyming words to build a frame of reference. Help students think of similar words they already know when confronted with an unfamiliar word. When attempting the word *yard*, say, "It ends like *hard* or *card*; now think of the beginning sound and tell me the word." Or say, "This word begins like *yellow*; use the same beginning sound in the new word." Follow a similar procedure to change the vowels in words: "What other words can you make by changing the vowel in *hit*?"
3. *Picture Match-Ups.* Pictures can be used in a variety of ways to improve phonic analysis, but again have students say and write the target sound each time:
    a) Show a picture and 2–3 words; have students select the word that begins or ends with the sound of the picture name;
    b) Show a row of pictures and have students select the pictures whose names begin or end alike;
    c) Show pictures with partial words; have students fill in the letters that complete the words that name the pictures; and
    d) Use index cards with pictures on the back representing the word on the front of the card.
4. *Sound Blending.* To teach blending of separate sounds, have students add a sound at a time to the beginning sound, as in *f _ _ _; fa _ _; fas _; fast.* Model the process and then have students repeat with you.
5. *Extra Practice.* • Pair students to practice substituting sounds using consonant and vowel wheels. • Tape stories, but pause as you delete a phonetically regular word every 2–3 sentences; have students listen and write the missing words. • Adapt ideas from Special Need 2.

26. USING STRUCTURAL ANALYSIS

DETECTION This may be a special skill need of students who:

- Are unfamiliar with prefixes and suffixes
- Have difficulty identifying word parts
- Appear confused about root words
- Do not recognize compound words or contractions
- Do not know where to divide words into syllables
- Also have difficulty with sight words and phonic skills (SN 24–25)

Description.   Structural analysis involves using the meaningful parts of words to decode the words. The application of meaning-based and self-monitoring strategies are particularly helpful in using structural analysis skills. The three major types of word parts generally included in the study of word structure include root words, inflectional endings, and affixes (prefixes and suffixes). In addition to these word parts, compound words, contractions, and syllabication are also studied. Structural skills are sometimes taught as a part of both word recognition and vocabulary development and are, therefore, considered to be of considerable importance.

Causation.   The most common cause of difficulty in using structural analysis as a decoding strategy is insufficient direct instruction and meaningful practice. A lack of adequate teaching and directed practice are responsible for many students not using structural analysis skills. Some of the students who have received instruction have been exposed to poor teaching practices such as hunting for little words in big ones, overreliance on phonic analysis, or too little stress on vocabulary development. Since the word parts should be taught as intact sight-word units, students who experience visual discrimination or visual memory problems may have problems mastering structural analysis skills. Special groups of students who may exhibit this special need are the teacher disabled, language disabled, mentally retarded, and visually impaired.

Implications.   For many students, structural analysis skills are more easily mastered than phonic or contextual analysis. The concrete nature of using words and word parts makes structural skills easier to teach and apply. Structural analysis skills are particularly important for students with auditory difficulties to master; when taught as sight units, these word parts can be used to partially compensate for less skilled use of phonic analysis. As a decoding strategy, use of structural analysis is much quicker than sounding out words and more easily understood than contextual skills. In many instances, structural skills are not emphasized until after phonic, context, and dictionary skills have been introduced. However, by teaching recognition and meanings of prefixes, suffixes, and root words, both word-recognition and word-meaning skills can be improved even as students begin to read.

CORRECTION Modify these strategies to meet students' learning needs.

1. *Premier Prefixes (or Supreme Suffixes).* Every 2–5 days, select a specific prefix or suffix for special instruction and direct use. Select a high-frequency affix that appears in printed materials being used during the week. Explain any special meaning along with underlining, highlighting, or calling attention to the affix by having students locate and point to the word part upon request. Present additional words containing the same affix and discuss the resulting meaning changes.

2. *Root-Word Find.* Teach students to look for root words by removing the common affixes and then identifying the root. Then have students determine the meaning of the root word and the affixes or inflectional endings. Discuss other affixes that could be added to the root word and the resulting meaning changes as well as other root words to which the word parts could be affixed. This type of analysis requires students to understand how to build a word from its root or base word.

3. *Matchmates.* Following a period of explanation and instructional application, give students groups of root words and prefixes and/or suffixes or contractions or compound words and their component words to match. Later, provide sentences in which the word parts have been omitted and ask students to either select or fill in an acceptable prefix or suffix or substitute a contraction or compound word. This can also be presented in game format using competing teams.

4. *Sight Parts.* Present common syllables as intact units to be mastered as sight words. Guide students to analyze known words and decide upon some important syllables, including affixes, that occur frequently in their texts. Discuss the meanings, if any, of the syllables as you model and then guide students to highlight or color-code their distinctive features and configurations. Have students pronounce the syllables as separate units, say their meanings, write them, spell them, and then pronounce and write the full words, again saying the total word meaning. Lead students to conclude syllabication and accent rules for words with these syllables.

5. *Proper Endings.* Provide instruction in determining 1–2 appropriate inflectional endings, such as *ed* or *s.* Then give students sentences requiring them to determine the appropriate ending according to word use. First, present this experience orally, using sentences on the board until students become accustomed to the activity. Contractions can be taught and reinforced in a similar manner.

6. *Extra Practice.* • Have students make a poster using 3 columns to show frequently occurring prefixes (or suffixes), their meanings, and sample words using the affix. • Give students pages from the newspaper and have them locate and circle 3–5 affixes. • Encourage the use of the dictionary to determine meanings of affixes or root words, syllabication, and accent. • Adapt strategies from Special Needs 24, 25, and 31.

27. USING CONTEXTUAL ANALYSIS

DETECTION This may be a special skill need of students who:

- Do not use surrounding text to decode unknown words
- Mispronounce many words when reading orally
- Rely too heavily upon sounding out words
- Are easily confused by long sentences
- Exhibit weak comprehension skills (SN 28– 34)

Description. Contextual analysis is as much a comprehension skill as a word-recognition or decoding strategy. As a word-recognition skill, it is probably the most efficient and effective, offering clues to meaning as well as pronunciation. The use of context to decode words requires students to understand other words around the problem word(s) in order to figure out meaning. Context involves a type of inferential thinking in which readers use what they understand to determine the meaning of what is left. Both semantic and syntactic clues are available for use in decoding other words and phrases.

Causation. A poorly developed meaning-based vocabulary, an inability to predict and infer, and a lack of meaningful practice using contextual analysis are all possible reasons for difficulty using context effectively. Students with an overall weak language background or a multilingual background often have difficulty using contextual analysis. In addition to language difficulties, the predictions and inferences required for contextual analysis may present problems for some students, especially the slow learners, learning disabled, and mentally retarded.

Implications. Using context is perhaps the word-recognition procedure most frequently applied by proficient readers. When used properly, context can help students determine both the pronunciations and the meanings of unfamiliar words. When teamed with sight-word recognition, phonic analysis, and structural analysis, contextual analysis is a powerful decoding tool. Unfortunately, too many beginning reading programs teach sight words and phonic analysis, followed by structural analysis, and finally, almost as an afterthought, use of context. Because all of the word-recognition skills should be presented and applied in meaningful context, contextual analysis should be taught as an integral part of word recognition and meaning from the very first day of reading instruction. The utility of contextual analysis is not confined to reading alone but is also important to mastering the content and concepts of all other subjects as well. Effective corrective instruction must include demonstrations, discussions, and explanations of the thinking strategies involved in predicting and verifying with context as well as encouragement to use context along with the other word-recognition skills.

CORRECTION Modify these strategies to meet students' learning needs.

1. *Oral Cloze.* To demonstrate and apply the concept of using context, have students complete sentences as you talk. Begin a statement and stop talking near the end of a sentence. Have students predict the words that could logically end your sentence. As a variation, delete words in listening activities or oral instructions; have students identify the missing words.

2. *Skip It.* When students confront an unknown word in text, tell them to "Skip it and come back after the sentence ends." If the word is not decoded by sentence end, have students listen as you read aloud the sentence with the word deleted. Then read the sentence aloud again, but pronounce only the initial sound of the word in question. If needed, reread the sentence, this time pronouncing the beginning (or prefix, if present) and ending sounds of the target word. Regularly use this routine to force the use of context.

3. *Probed Questioning.* Questioning to guide students toward using what they already know can help them interpret unknown words and meanings. Ask direct questions requiring students to focus their attention on difficult phrases or words. Base the questions on portions of a sentence they already understand, and word them so that students must use the known information to help guess or predict the word meanings.

4. *Leveled Cloze.* The use of cloze-type formats for improving the use of contextual analysis is a widely accepted practice. Beginning with the easiest, these represent several formats by varying degrees of difficulty according to the deletion formats and the amount of clues provided:

    a. Our car (walked, tumbled) down the hill.
    b. Our car t _ _ _ _ ed down the hill.
    c. Our car t _ _ _ _ _ _ down the hill.
    e. Our car t _____ down the hill.
    f. Our car _____ down the hill.

5. *Assisted Cloze.* Some students will need an assisted cloze format. Retype selections from passages; replace 3–8 key words with the initial letter, blend or digraph, and a number of blanks equal to the number of letters in the missing word. For *th _ _* format, students may also need the correct word choices provided at the *t _ _* of the page or on the *chalkb _ _ _ _*.

6. *Extended Cloze.* Use storyframes, maxicloze, or extended cloze to involve students in first reading or listening to a short passage. Next have them use what they remember to fill in with their own words a cloze activity that is a reprint of the passage but with key words deleted.

7. *Extra Practice.* • Have students develop Extended Cloze selections for younger students. • Record short passages on audiotape and delete an ending statement; have students listen and make up an ending. • Present 3–5 concept words from a short passage; have students read, circle each key word, and then underline the parts of the passage that help explain or describe the meaning of the key words. • Adapt ideas from Special Need 31.

28. READING ORALLY

DETECTION This may be a special skill need of students who:

- Cannot answer comprehension questions after reading orally
- Read word by word and do not phrase by thought units
- Mispronounce or substitute many words
- Guess at unknown words
- Omit, insert, or repeat words and phrases
- Read too fast or too slow
- Seldom self-correct oral errors according to context (SN 27)

Description. Good oral reading is characterized by satisfactory pronunciation and phrasing, a moderate rate, and evidence of understanding after reading aloud. Acceptable oral reading includes demonstrated performance of both decoding and comprehension skills. Thus, students must also understand and recall what they read aloud. (The more specific skills of literal, inferential, and critical comprehension are discussed later in this chapter, SN 32–34.) The purposes for having students read aloud include to entertain, to inform, to share, and to use as a vehicle to teach silent reading as well as to diagnose reading needs.

Causation. Most students learn to read through an oral process involving an emphasis on decoding and correct pronunciation. Students who have to struggle to decode the words often overlook or lose comprehension. Incorrect oral production of text is often caused by insufficient sight vocabulary, inadequate use of word-attack skills, lack of self-monitoring strategies, fear of embarrassment, or carelessness. Because so much of beginning reading instruction focuses on oral word pronunciation, comprehension skills may be slighted, creating an imbalance between decoding and comprehension performance. Some students become "word callers," fluently saying the words but understanding little. Conversely, a few students make numerous errors as they read aloud yet understand what they read. Special groups of students who may have difficulty reading aloud with understanding include the language different, teacher disabled, hearing impaired, language disabled, learning disabled, and speech disordered.

Implications. Instruction in oral reading must stress not only pronunciation and phrasing but also the extraction of meaning. Routine oral reading in which comprehension does not occur can hardly be justified. Both developmental and corrective instruction in oral reading should be explicitly purposeful: The teacher must conduct the activities for legitimate instructional purposes and then give the oral readers specific purposes for reading aloud.

CORRECTION Modify these strategies to meet students' learning needs.

1. *Purposeful Oral Reading.* Define your instructional purpose for conducting each oral reading experience. Have each student silently preview the part he or she will read orally. Give the readers a specific purpose for reading aloud: "Read the part that answers the question," "Read this paragraph the way you think Jerry said it," or "Read the parts that prove your answer." If more than 1 student is involved, give the listeners a purpose: "Listen to see why Annette was so tired," "Listen to find out about Jorenda's new toy," or "As Holly reads, think of a good comprehension question to ask your peers."

2. *As I Recall.* Before oral reading experiences, tell students that you will want them to retell at least 1 important idea after they read or listen. After each reading, ask the reader to retell 1 idea. Then have each listener add an idea until the passage is retold. To extend the activity, then guide the students to summarize the passage.

3. *Mini-Choral Reading.* To improve phrasing and tempo, have pairs of students select a book that is easy for both to read. Say that they will be reading aloud in unison to learn to read more smoothly. Demonstrate by reading aloud several passages with them; have students follow your model to read aloud in unison for 5-minute sessions each day until fluency improves.

4. *Early Predictions.* Conduct a discussion about a story prior to having students read orally. Provide background information and a partial explanation of the story line. Then have each student guess what will happen in the story and explain the prediction. Along with predictions, you can also help students make up titles for the stories based on their predictions. Ask students to write their titles on the board and then correct their titles after reading or listening to the story.

5. *Oral Captions.* Videotaped-captioned TV shows designed for the hearing impaired. Use these without sound for individual or group reading experiences. Later, replay each tape with sound for verification and reinforcement.

6. *Extra Practice.* • Have students read short stories and paragraphs and make up prereading questions for others to use before they read the selections; if writing is a problem, students can dictate their questions; if reading is a problem, have students listen to a partner read and then make up prereading questions. • Prior to reading aloud for peers, permit students to use a tape recorder to practice. • Adapt word-recognition strategies from Special Needs 24–27.

29. READING SILENTLY

DETECTION This may be a special skill need of students who:

- Cannot answer questions about text read silently
- Subvocalize while reading silently
- Understand more when reading orally than when reading silently
- Are easily distracted when reading silently
- Take longer to finish reading than most other classmates
- Frequently complain about the length of reading assignments
- Seldom read silently for pleasure or recreation (SN 30)

Description. Silent reading involves the decoding function of identifying words and phrases in a meaningful sense and then responding by understanding overall concepts, ideas, and supporting facts. This requires both receptive and responsive processes as readers attempt to search, verify, skim, and scan printed materials. Most students learn to read silently after learning to read orally, the less efficient of the two reading modes. Silent comprehension proficiency is typically judged by the quantity and quality of information the readers recall and interpret after reading.

Causation. Unsatisfactory silent comprehension can result from inadequate word-recognition skills, limited vocabulary or background experiences, inattentiveness, poor motivation, lack of meaningful practice, and ineffective teaching. For some students, silent reading is a skill left to chance or at best to be developed on an independent basis. In many instances, students are left to practice reading silently with little or no direct monitoring or guidance. Lack of purpose and interest as well as the use of reading materials that are too difficult for students' skill levels also interfere with silent comprehension. Students who are easily distracted often have problems concentrating and staying on-task during silent reading. A few students appear to need the auditory input of oral reading in order to understand. Special groups of students who may evidence this skill need are the teacher disabled, visually impaired, behavior disordered, or learning disabled.

Implications. Oral reading is expected of beginning readers, but as they progress to content above the second-grade level, curricular demands to read silently gradually increase. As students progress through the academic curriculum, demands for independent learning, relying heavily on silent reading, increase in all subjects. Unless students are able to read silently with understanding, reading as well as academic performance in general will suffer. Instruction to correct silent comprehension needs should begin with easy reading materials that are below the level of the students' sight vocabulary, word-analysis skills, and oral or listening comprehension skills.

CORRECTION Modify these strategies to meet students' learning needs.

1. *Silent Purposes.* After building and discussing the vocabulary and concepts needed to understand a passage, always give students a purpose for reading: "Read the next part to answer this question," "Find out why the duck waddled," "Find three happy words," or "Just for fun." Identify any elements that distract students while reading and then either eliminate or minimize the distractions. Break text into short, manageable units, gradually increasing passage length and difficulty as students progress.

2. *Sentence Detectives.* Write 5–8 sentences dealing with a familiar story. Before having each sentence read silently, provide an oral statement in the form of a prediction or question. Have the students listen to your inquiry and then read a sentence in order to respond: "Was this a wonderful experience? Why or why not?" or "Is this event important or not? Why?" "Could you have done better than Karen? How?" Later on, use sentences about stories the students have not previously read. As a more difficult application of Sentence Detectives, have students also read the inquiry statements silently before reading the main story sentences.

3. *Answers First.* Before assigning silent reading, give students 2–5 answers. After their reading is completed, have them construct questions that match the prereading answers you provided. The answers can be to literal as well as to inferential questions, providing you present implied answers (e.g., unstated effects, logical conclusions, etc.)

4. *Facts, Please.* Present 2–3 facts from a passage; then have students read silently to decide which ones are from the passage and which ones are not. To extend the activity, give students 3 choices of titles before they silently read the passage or page. After reading, have them select the best title and justify their answers. Later, you may want them to generate their own titles. Title selection and construction can assist students to identify important and general concepts during silent reading.

5. *Word Guides.* Before silent reading, have students scan the passage and write each major heading and subheading. This is particularly appropriate for use in expository texts (e.g., history, social studies, science, or health). After copying the headings, have them read each section and write a phrase and 2–3 words that tell what the section is about. After reading, discuss each section and have students assist as you write each subheading, summary phrase, and key words on the board. Use a talk-through procedure to model how to verify and refine the most important words and phrases. Then teach students to simplify subheadings and captions for pictures and drawings as they read. This can be done as a prereading or postreading experience to learn more about the concepts involved.

6. *Extra Practice.* • As a special favor, ask students to silently read a chapter or story and then tape 5 good comprehension questions (and answers) for peers. • Adapt ideas from Special Needs 6–8, 28, and 32–34.

30. READING FOR PLEASURE

DETECTION This may be a special skill need of students who:

- Seldom read unassigned books and other materials
- Show little interest in printed materials
- Make excuses for not reading
- Complain about having to read
- Have difficulty comprehending as they read (SN 28, 29, 31–34)

Description. Pleasure reading can be described as recreational reading, free read-
ing, private reading, or personal reading. Regardless of title, the key factor is the students' enjoyment of reading. Students who find reading
pleasurable are more likely to voluntarily read because they want to
read, thus improving their reading skills and becoming lifelong readers.
Reading guidance is often required to help students select books they
might enjoy. Incentives, class time, teacher modeling, easy access to
books, and self-selection are useful for encouraging pleasure reading.

Causation. Many students are not accustomed to reading without accountability.
A lack of student interest in personal reading may stem from a lack of
in-school opportunities, insufficient numbers of good books available
for reading, and a general lack of teacher valuing of the process. Many
teachers project reading as a skill-based, lesson-oriented experience that
takes place only at a specific time in a certain corner of the room; these
same teachers fail to mention that reading can be fun. In some classes,
reading is even used as a punitive measure whereby additional pages,
chapters, or book reports are assigned to punish inappropriate classroom behaviors. Students who must constantly struggle to decode and
then comprehend reading assignments, who have primarily experienced
reading as highly structured activities using a basal reader, and who seldom see parents or teachers read for recreation are not likely to choose
to read for fun. In addition to students who tend to avoid reading because
of their overall weak reading skills, special groups of students who may
not voluntarily read are the disadvantaged, culturally or language different, teacher disabled, behavior disordered, and language or learning
disabled.

Implications. In addition to providing enjoyable school experiences, the importance of reading for pleasure resides in the possibilities for improving
reading skills. Students who are taught the joys of reading are more
likely to read often; the more students read, the more their reading skills
improve. For reading to be fun, it must be easy enough for students to attend to the content, not the mechanics. Guide students to select materials
in which they can comprehend approximately 95% of the content. Emphasize enjoyment and minimize the threat of evaluating and reporting.
Drilling and skilling are of little value unless students understand the
joy and value of reading.

CORRECTION Modify these strategies to meet students' learning needs.

1. *Sustained Reading.* Set aside 5–15 minutes every day for silent reading in a book personally selected with your guidance to insure ease of reading for enjoyment. Distractions should be controlled while all students and teachers participate. No evaluation or report should be required. The single requirement is that everyone reads.
2. *Story Features.* On a daily basis, provide a 5–10-minute feature from a portion of a good book by reading orally to the class. Afterwards, have the book available for students to finish reading individually.
3. *Book Bargains.* Classroom libraries and well-stocked school libraries are necessary for pleasure reading to become a realistic goal. A number of book clubs offer teachers free books for classroom libraries in return for disseminating the publisher's order forms to class members. Ask students to request parent permission to donate to the class library any books that the children no longer read. Inside the front cover of these books, mount a book plate that displays the donor's name and the date. Enlist extra help from a school parent/teacher organization, a local business, or hold a book fair or school program to raise money to purchase books. Most adults will be glad to help support efforts to buy books. Be sure to seek the suggestions of the school librarian and school administrators as you plan any fundraising effort.
4. *Book Clubs.* Establish a classroom book club. Take trips to the library as a group to locate, read, and share good books. Have students write positive letters to their favorite authors in care of the publisher. Group letters should be sent rather than individual letters except in special circumstances. Many authors will respond to questions about characters, new books, and their interests in particular types of writing. Make your book club responsible for a bulletin board in a main hall of the school each month or 6-week period.
5. *Reading Incentives.* Even older students can be motivated by the use of stars, stickers, listing of names, prizes, and group rewards. Progress charts and other numerical or score-keeping systems can be used with some students. However, public displays of the number of books read by each student and rewards for the most books read defeats the purpose of positive incentives. Incentives are motivating only when they are attainable by all participants. This means completed paragraphs, pages, chapters, or entire books can be used as completion of a successful reading effort. Group rewards may be used (a special privilege or ice cream treat for all) if 100% participation is maintained during a specified period.
6. *Extra Practice.* • Take candid pictures of students reading and post them on a bulletin board. • Have a special rocking chair, beanbag, pillow, filled tire, or bathtub in the room just for personal reading. • Have students share a taped interview with a peer about a favorite book. • Adapt ideas from Special Need 9.

31. UNDERSTANDING WORD MEANINGS

DETECTION This may be a special skill need of students who:

- Display a limited listening, speaking, reading, and writing vocabulary
- Frequently miss vocabulary questions
- Often ask the meanings of words
- Know only one meaning for most words
- Exhibit little knowledge of word relationships
- Frequently request help pronouncing words (SN 24–26)
- Do not appear to use contextual analysis when reading (SN 27)

Description. An understanding of word meanings is essential to skilled word recognition and comprehension. Such understanding facilitates students' active involvement in predicting and interpreting meanings based upon usage and reader knowledge. All three major skill areas of word recognition, phonic, structural, and contextual analysis, contribute to the development of a strong reading and writing vocabulary. Not only must students understand the actual words of specific passages but they must also master strategies for figuring out meanings on their own as well as have the desire to do so. A constantly expanding vocabulary is an important part of progress in all areas of the language arts curriculum.

Causation. Underdeveloped meaning vocabularies often result from limited experiences speaking and listening to appropriate language models. Inadequate direct instruction or stimulation, insufficient concrete examples and background experiences, isolated skill practice, and too few opportunities to stretch their word knowledge also limit vocabulary growth. Although knowledge or word meanings is a typical academic strength of many gifted students, many groups of special learners may exhibit an academic weakness in this area. Among the students who are more likely than others to exhibit sparse vocabularies are the culturally and language different, slow learners, teacher disabled, hearing impaired, language disabled, learning disabled, mentally retarded, physically or medically handicapped, and speech disordered.

Implications. Inadequate knowledge of word meanings is readily apparent in the classroom because of the interference with students' performance across the language arts curriculum. For many students, vocabulary development rarely takes place unless direct instruction is provided on a regular basis. Some students are able to maintain adequate reading progress through the first years of school and then, as vocabulary demands increase dramatically in subject-area textbooks, their general achievement seems to fall rapidly. To develop and maintain a strong vocabulary, students should receive instruction that involves all facets of the language arts. To achieve long-term mastery, activities that include both reading and writing are particularly important.

CORRECTION Modify these strategies to meet students' learning needs.

1. *OWD.* As a simple but effective plan, introduce or have students select at least One Word a Day to master. Each word should be pronounced, discussed, used orally, written, read in context, and incorporated into other lessons during the day. Allot a few minutes each day for small groups to discuss the new word and then decide on a new one for the next day. You may want to teach OWD on Monday through Thursday but review the 4 words on Friday.

2. *Word-Mastery Guidelines.* To turn boring, ineffective vocabulary lessons into meaningful ones, follow these do's and don't's:

    a. Don't have students look up words in a dictionary, copy the definitions and use each word in a sentence. Such practice has been shown to be little more effective than doing nothing at all. For many students, these are boring, negative experiences and may even impede progress.

    b. Do introduce new words in context, use visual aids, and, when appropriate, discuss multiple meanings.

    c. Do combine phonic, structural, and contextual analysis training along with the meaning-based emphasis. The word-recognition strategies help reinforce student retention as well as build word-recognition skills.

    d. Don't have students memorize meanings of words; instead, as you discuss a word, have the students decide how they can personally use the word in their own speech and writing. Then, recognize and reward students' use of the target words in other lessons.

    e. Do close each lesson by involving students in some form of oral or written experience that requires using each new word 2–5 times.

    f. Do use frequent review periods for activities with new words that cause students to elaborate, combine, or reduce concepts in sentence form.

    g. Do encourage the use of personal language logs, word banks, lists, posters, journal writing, and other self motivating ideas to help document progress or encourage word usage.

3. *Mapping, Webbing, and Remembering.* Whenever possible, present new words according to their relationships with known words. As noted in Chapter 1, involving students in classification activities not only builds the conceptual framework for understanding the words but also deepens and reinforces their understanding of the interrelated terms.

4. *Concept Analysis List.* When presenting new words or using them in text, present or have students create topical headings under which to place concepts or characteristics. In a science text, headings such as these could be used.

	plant	mineral	animal
goat			
tree			

5. *Extra Practice.* • Have students use a dictionary and thesaurus to contrast word meanings. • Ask students to develop word puzzles and matching activities for peers. • Adapt ideas from Special Needs 11, 26, and 27.

32. UNDERSTANDING LITERAL INFORMATION

DETECTION This may be a special skill need of students who:

- Have difficulty answering the who, what, when, and where questions
- Often forget details and general information
- Remember the facts but not in order
- Cannot quickly locate the answers in the book
- Must reread to remember information
- Have a limited listening, speaking, and reading vocabulary (SN 3, 11, 31)

Description. Although comprehension is a thought process including more than any one or two discrete skills, it is often necessary to isolate specific skills for instructional purposes. Instruction in literal comprehension is primarily concerned with helping students read or listen and remember directly stated or text-explicit information. This requires recognition of the details as they occur and the recall of them after reading, often in the sequence of occurrence. Some experts consider literal types of information to be the easiest of the three levels of comprehension to teach. However, some students may actually be able to accurately respond to inferential or critical questions but not literal questions. In most cases, all three levels of response should be taught, and specific intervention should be provided for one or more areas when needed.

Causation. Poor overall reading skills, including word recognition and vocabulary knowledge or a lack of concentration, are often responsible for problems in understanding literal information. Frequently, students forced to read materials that are too difficult do not understand or forget the facts. A reading rate that is too fast or too slow also interferes with the recall of literal information, as does inadequate sorting of relevant facts. A general weakness in sequential memory may cause students to exhibit difficulty in sequencing events. Gifted students are sometimes so hampered by their intensity and search for hidden meaning that they miss some of the obvious details as they read. Students with weak language skills or hearing problems may find this task particularly difficult.

Implications. Problems here affect overall comprehension and thus total reading progress. This difficulty is likely to impede progress in other academic areas as well, particularly those that are fact laden, such as social studies and science. Corrective instruction must include modeling, explanation, discussion, and application. Students must develop a personal system of applying prior knowledge, confirming, and monitoring their reading. It is important for special learners to initially focus on understanding the facts in sentences and short paragraphs instead of story-length material. Once progress is made, the passage length can be gradually lengthened.

CORRECTION Modify these strategies to meet students' learning needs.

1. *Using Known Information.* Provide instruction to help students verbalize what they know about a topic before listening or reading about the topic. Then after a few sentences, repeat the process by asking, "What does this tell us about . . .?" By teaching students to self-question, they learn to monitor their reading as it occurs.

2. *Cut-Ups.* Print sentences on sentence strips or index cards; then cut the sentences into phrases or 2–3 word segments. Have students arrange the pieces so the sentence makes sense, each time reading aloud their choices to confirm. Once confirmed, have students write each sentence in correct order. Use discarded texts for the same purposes, cutting sentences into phrases or separating paragraphs for students to reorder. Mount each segment so that students rely on text instead of shape.

3. *Find the Facts.* Print sentences from a passage on the chalkboard and underline 2–3 facts, one of which is unrelated to the material. Ask students to read a brief passage to determine which fact does not fit; then read aloud their choices to confirm the fit.

4. *Given or Not?* Give students a list of 2–6 facts from a passage, and ask them to listen or read to decide if each fact is or is not stated in the material. A list of sequenced facts can be used for the same purpose. Have them reread or listen again, highlighting the facts as they occur.

5. *Supporting Details.* Provide 2–3 details that are related to a topic statement in a paragraph. Have students use the details and decide which statement is a topic sentence that the details relate to.

6. *Factual Recitation.* Ask students to read or listen to a paragraph or short selection. Then have them retell 2–4 major facts that were given in the material.

7. *Self-Generated W's.* Begin by asking students who, what, and where questions before and after they read. Have them underline the facts as they occur in text; then suggest that they begin asking and answering these 3 types of fact questions in their own mind as they read. Next, ask students to read, and before discussing the content, have the students state their W's.

8. *Unfinished Sentences.* A modified cloze format can be used after reading or listening is completed. Provide 2–6 sentences in which specific factual information has been omitted. Leave a blank for students to fill in the missing details. The nearer to the end of a sentence you leave a blank, the easier it will usually be to fill in.

9. *Extra Practice.* • After some students learn to question themselves using the 3 W's, have them show a friend how to do the same. • Provide paragraphs cut from consumable text and have students read and underline no more than 2–4 important facts in each paragraph. • Ask students to rewrite stories or paragraphs and leave out unnecessary facts or unrelated information. • Adapt strategies from Special Needs 3, 11, 27, and 31.

33. UNDERSTANDING INFERENTIAL INFORMATION

DETECTION This may be a special skill need of students who:

- Have difficulty answering inference questions
- Cannot interpret text-implicit information
- Are unable to identify main ideas
- Have difficulty concluding unstated passage events
- Cannot predict what is about to occur in text
- Have problems linking cause and effect
- Exhibit weak literal comprehension skills (SN 32)

Description. Inferential comprehension involves students' use of information they already know, adding information from the text, and then making decisions about implied information that are either logical or best guesses. The ability to infer from printed information is closely related to interpreting oral language, gestures, or nonverbal information people display. Inference is not necessarily a right or wrong determination but one of best choice, given certain information. Among the types of inferences that may be required are finding the main idea, drawing conclusions, predicting events, and determining cause and effect.

Causation. Several of the same causes of literal difficulties can be attributed to inferential comprehension as well: inadequate word recognition skills, limited vocabulary knowledge, insufficient understanding of literal information, or the use of text that is above students' overall reading achievement level. Additionally, limited mental ability, environmental factors including noise and interruptions, limited background knowledge, and an overdependence upon oral reading can be cited as potential causes for poor inferential comprehension. Special groups of students who may exhibit this special need include those with experience and language deficits, as well as the slow learners, learning disabled, and mentally retarded.

Implications. Literal and inferential comprehension are among the most basic of the comprehension tasks. Making inferences is difficult because students cannot always refer back to a word or phrase as "the" answer. Some experts have equated inferential comprehension to making educated guesses based upon the available information. Problems inferring may interfere with such tasks as critical comprehension, speaking concisely and writing succinctly, finding similarities and differences, summarizing, and understanding math problems, as well as with overall performance in science and social studies. Corrective instruction must begin with the provision of additional background or prereading information to help students better understand what they are about to read. Purposes for reading must be clearly stated and matched to the ability level of the students.

CORRECTION Modify these strategies to meet students' learning needs.

1. *Riddle Me's.* Use riddles to illustrate how to infer. Have students listen to and then read a riddle. Talk through the process of sorting out possible answers, meanings, and making educated guesses based upon the information. Continue modeling and practice until students progress.

2. *Inference Picks.* Give students a short paragraph to read or listen to. Then provide 2 statements, one reflecting a fact from the text, the other reflecting information not stated but inferred from the material. Ask students to identify the factual statement and the one based upon inference. Reread and then discuss how the inference was determined. Ask students to tell how they came up with their answers.

3. *Sentence Combining.* Using recently read material, print 2–3 short sentences on the board. Ask students to combine the sentences into 1–2 longer sentences that will convey the same meaning. Model the process using several sets of cause/effect or main-idea sentences; then have students help you combine sentences.

4. *Instant Inference.* Using headlines, phrases, or titles, ask students to determine the stated (literal) and implied (inferential) meaning of 2–6 items. For example, have students give the stated and implied meanings of headlines such as these: "Tiger Born to Man with Two Heads" or "Father of Six Shoots Hole in One."

5. *Broadway Questions.* Inform students that literal questions are very narrow and require facts directly from the text; use examples. Next, explain that questions can be very broad and require more than a factual or yes/no response. Broadway Questions involve much more thinking and responding, and they cannot be answered using only textual information. Guide students to develop Broadway Questions by providing the beginning part of inference questions such as: "Why do you think that Missy . . .?" "What will Angel say when . . .?" or "What caused Jerry to . . .?" Have students finish the question and supply the answer, first orally, and then in writing.

6. *Sarcastic No-No's.* Although teachers avoid the use of inappropriate sarcastic comments, students often use such language. When this occurs, discuss the inference involved and relate it to interpreting text that students have recently read. Also consider having students suggest sarcastic comments to insert in text as they read.

7. *Inappropriate Questions.* Apply inference to study questions and everyday statements. For example, a friend just ran in from outside and looks soaked. Someone asks, "Is it raining?" or "How is the weather?" or "What have you been doing?" Point out that these questions require inferences.

8. *Extra Practice.* • Ask students to read a lesson or story a day or so before classmates and construct 2–3 Broadway Questions to use with the class. • Tape commercials and have students listen and determine the overall inference(s) made in the advertisement.

34. READING CRITICALLY

DETECTION This may be a special skill need of students who:

- Are unable to make judgments from reading
- Find evaluating or analyzing content difficult
- Have difficulty differentiating fact, fiction, and opinion
- Accept the validity of text without question
- Do not listen critically (SN 8)
- Have weak inferential comprehension skills (SN 33)

Description. Critical comprehension is often included in discussions of thinking skills and problem solving. To read critically, students must rely heavily on experience and prior knowledge. Critical reading is often considered to be an extension of inferential level thinking, although no such static categories can be documented. In addition to making predictions or judgments, evaluating content (e.g., using propaganda techniques, recognizing fact and opinion) and making creative or application responses to questions are also included under this category. Students must interact with the text and critique its worth, validity, and true message. Critical comprehension includes reading *beyond* the lines to evaluate them and reading *behind* the lines to evaluate the author's techniques.

Causation. Perhaps the single greatest cause of critical comprehension weaknesses is the lack of direct instruction. Unfortunately, most classroom instruction focuses on literal comprehension and occasionally inferential comprehension. At best, attempts to build critical comprehension skills often consist of tacking on a few critical questions or using the supplementary activities in basals labeled "extension" or "extra practice." Critical comprehension involves very sophisticated thinking skills. Students who have low mental abilities, poor general comprehension, or unsatisfactory word-recognition skills will likely experience difficulty reading critically.

Implications. Critical comprehension is considered by many to be the highest level of comprehension. In fact, in some reading materials, critical reading is treated as a separate skill area and is listed after word-recognition, comprehension, and study skills. Regardless of its placement in a scope and sequence design, except for the gifted, most students continue to receive little instruction in its use. Because this is a real-life reading skill, all students need specific instruction in critical comprehension. To become active, thinking, questioning readers and listeners, many students must be directly taught specific strategies to critically comprehend. Corrective instruction should begin with strategies for evaluating text that is very easy for the students and must include guidance for developing specific criteria with which to evaluate text.

CORRECTION Modify these strategies to meet students' learning needs.

1. *Prediction Cues.* Show students a title or picture for a story. Ask them to predict what the story will be about. Encourage explanation of the information used to make their predictions, and have them read or listen to the story to confirm or revise original predictions. Later, have them tell or write the story as they predicted it or the way they would prefer it and then rate the stories as a group activity.
2. *Personal Endings.* Before finishing a story, stop and ask students to provide an oral or written ending that they think makes sense. Have students share and defend their endings and then compare the differences with the original story. Then, discuss the 2–3 best endings, thinking aloud and listing the factors that contribute to "best."
3. *Raters.* As students read or listen to text, have them rate the content. To differentiate fact from fiction, have them rate each statement as "yes, "no," or "maybe," according to reality; use a similar rating plan to distinguish fact from opinion. Have students discuss and justify each response.
4. *Is That a Fact?* After listening or reading a selection, give students 3–6 statements that are facts or opinions. Ask students to determine if each statement is a fact or opinion according to the text and to prove and discuss reasons for their answers. Use the fact/opinion statements before reading as advance organizers; reconsider them after reading or listening.
5. *Provoking Propaganda.* Analyze the types of propaganda techniques used in events in class or advertisements on TV or in print. Have students discuss the type in use. Five of the most popular propaganda techniques are these:
    a. *Bandwagon*—"Everyone is doing it, so why not you?"
    b. *Plain Folks*—"This is old Humble Henry asking for your support. Elect one of the real people to office."
    c. Testimonial—"Two out of three experts recommend our product." (Testimonials can be given by famous or not-so-famous people.)
    d. *Glittering Generalities*—"Our appliances have sparkling chrome handles, porcelain finishes, deluxe controls; and best of all, you'll see pride in our machines."
    e. *Transfer*—"Consider the freedom, security, and piece of mind you could have. Better sleep comes with Protecto Services."
6. *Slanted Headlines.* After completing a lesson or story, ask students to develop 2–3 good newspaper headlines for the lesson; restate their headlines to alter the meaning; then discuss how the changes affect meaning. Or give students 2 possible slanted headlines for a story; have them listen or read the story to select the headline that fits.
7. *Extra Practice.* • Have students develop fact and opinion statements for an upcoming lesson to quiz peers. • Ask students to list their own criteria for evaluating text. • Adapt ideas from Special Needs 8 and 33.

35. BUILDING STUDY HABITS

DETECTION This may be a special skill need of students who:

- Often do not complete or are late with assignments
- Perform better during lessons than on tests
- Appear disorganized when working in class
- Do not apply a systematic study technique
- Have difficulty summarizing and taking notes (SN 36)

Description. The three major components for building effective study habits include organizing for study, previewing information, and then systematically applying study techniques. Metacognition also plays an important
role as students monitor their knowledge, determine the explanations
they need, and attend to appropriate materials. Organizing for study involves the methodical arrangement of self and lesson content for study
and may include outlining, summary writing, interpreting graphic aids,
and using reference sources. In many respects, previewing content is an
integral part of organizing for study as students quickly survey the content to anticipate and gather general information as well as decide upon
the study props they need. Study techniques involve several sequential
procedures that, when applied sytematically, enable students to understand and recall lesson content.

Causation. The single greatest cause of poor study habits is a lack of direct instruction and application in textbook materials. Many teachers present
the content and then evaluate the students' knowledge, omitting the critical step of guiding and monitoring students to work through assignments. Some students are unwilling to spend the time necessary to keep
up with assignments, notes, and required reading. Lack of encouragement at home and an improper study environment also interfere with
study. Numerous special students evidence specific needs in all of the
study skills.

Implications. Many students recognize the need for systematic study only on the
day before a test, too late to approach the content methodically. Unless
teachers routinely guide the development of study habits and pace learning experiences to facilitate mastery of content and systematic study,
students are not likely to develop the study habits necessary to improve
academic performance in all areas.

CORRECTION Modify these strategies to meet students' learning needs.

1. *Study Systems.* Select a study system such as PRE (see Activity 4) and teach students to use it regularly. The manner in which you introduce a study system is critical to its implementation. The introduction should include these elements: a) a discussion of his or her learning style with each student; b) a description and explanation of the benefits of the system; c) modeling of the mechanics and thinking procedures; d) naming of the procedures by the students as they mimic your model; and e) meaningful practice activities, beginning with easy content before progressing to more difficult tasks.

2. *Practice Assignments.* Give students simulated assignments, and then help them develop a checklist for accomplishing each task. Ask such questions as: What materials will you need? How much time will be necessary? Where should you look first? The resulting checklist should include basic materials, resources, time allotment, procedures, and study approach. Then, have students apply their checklist to studying actual assignments.

3. *Previewing.* Give 2–5 preview statements about a chapter or story. Explain that Previewing is similar to seeing a preview for a TV program; it is used to predict what will happen next. Have students read previews, stating orally or in writing their predictions of the content. Have them discuss the information they used to make their predictions. Later, compare predictions to the text itself.

4. *PRE as a Study System.* Previewing, Reading, and Expressing (PRE) is one of the easiest study systems to use. Explain and then have students apply each of the 3 steps several times. Use an overhead projector or chalkboard to make such explanations more meaningful. *Previewing* requires students to read headings, look for questions, summaries, illustrations, and important vocabulary. The second step, *Reading,* can be broken into 1-page segments as students learn to read to verify information predicted during previewing. Ask students to monitor their progress as they look for certain ideas or answers. Use teacher-directed talk-through to show self-questioning during silent reading. *Expressing* requires students to talk about, or rehearse, what they read.

5. *Study Center.* Set aside a special table and chair with a dictionary, thesaurus, extra paper, and even a special light if necessary. Have students sign up for a time for uninterrupted use of the special Study Center. Encourage students to study in a similar quiet place at home.

6. *Extra Practice.* • After the oral expression portion of PRE, have students write down ideas that were expressed after reading. • Have students teach a peer how to use PRE as a study plan. • Give pairs of students a syllabus and schedule for a subject to keep track of deadlines and assignments; have them make a study schedule that includes the elements of Practice Assignments. • Have pairs of students take turns previewing upcoming assignments, as in Activity 3. • Adapt ideas from Special Needs 36–38.

36. NOTETAKING AND SUMMARY WRITING

DETECTION This may be a special skill need of students who:

- Have problems taking notes from reading
- Cannot take notes while listening
- Have trouble stating or writing a summary
- Have difficulty organizing information
- Cannot outline text
- Do not apply a systematic study technique (SN 35)

Description. Notetaking and summary writing can also involve mapping, outlining, thinking, and determining main ideas and details. Both are important study aids as well as tools for conducting research and writing papers and speeches. Outlining and mapping help students maintain organization within their writing. Revision and expansion are the parts of the notetaking process that occur as the original notes are rewritten. Related skills include critical listening and specific and general comprehension skills.

Causation. In order to be able to take notes, students must develop listening comprehension, outlining, writing vocabulary, and general comprehension skills sufficiently to enable them to record information for later use. Weaknesses in any of these skills interfere with students' abilities to summarize and take notes. Books that are poorly written and teachers who present disorganized lessons without stated objectives, modeling, and clear directions make notetaking difficult. Many students have simply not been taught how to outline, summarize, or take notes. The tasks are so complex and difficult that some students are unwilling to exert the effort and give up. So many variables and skills are involved that special students in many categories tend to experience difficulty mastering notetaking and summarizing.

Implications. Reading assigned material before it is discussed makes outlining and taking notes easier. Taking notes after reading is different than taking notes while listening. Notes taken while listening usually need to be reviewed and expanded. Students should be taught to listen for key phrases and vocabulary so that they can go back later and fill in information gaps. Notes taken after or during reading do not always need to be rewritten, since students have the time to reword, condense, and highlight without the pressure of lost ideas or key points because a speaker moved onto the next point. An emphasis on process and product will help students learn the importance of study habits. Evaluating outlines, draft copies, and notes allows students to receive credit as they go along in addition to a grade for a final product. Instruction in summarizing and notetaking should begin as early as possible and should be integrated with instruction in all the language arts. Many of the suggestions provided in the listening section may be adapted for developing outlining and notetaking skills while listening.

CORRECTION Modify these strategies to meet students' learning needs.

1. *Easy Notes.* Use an overhead projector to demonstrate one way to take notes while listening. Use a half-page format to first take down ideas on the left and then go back later and fill in more details on the right beside the topic. Have your students take notes on their own paper as you write.

2. *Jumbled Facts.* Give students a list of 4–6 topics, concepts, phrases, or facts. Next, have them read a paragraph and decide how the order and/or classification of topics should be arranged. Ask students to write an outline; then take notes. Compare the results among the class members.

3. *Basic Outlining.* Begin by giving students a partially completed outline containing 25% of the information needed to complete the spaces provided. More information can be included, depending upon the ability of your students. Keep the format simple by including only major headings and perhaps 1–2 subcategories. Model the process using the chalkboard or overhead projector. Next, have students fill in another partially completed outline. Gradually decrease the amount of information provided on the outline. Students should then be able to determine their own categories. Word or phrase outlines can also be used.

4. *Concept Maps.* Begin by developing a concept map with students, using information from a textbook they are currently reading. Use a circle and print a title or major topic in the center. Then draw lines like wheel spokes out from the circle's hub and place key concepts or subtopics at the ends of the lines. Below these words go facts and related details about the subtopics. Like the maps and webs described in Chapter 1, the completed map shows students the general organization and relationships of the material. Concept maps are like outlines in a different form. Partially completed maps can be used like the partially completed outlines in Activity 3 until students are able to construct their own. Have students use a completed map to write a basic outline.

5. *Summary Soup.* Pass out 2–5 short paragraphs or sentences on index cards. Ask students to read their information orally, and have the students write a group summary using the information. Demonstrate the process with the students 2–3 times before assigning this task. During the guided lessons, emphasize how to go about combining or elaborating information by first determining a major concept and then using related ideas or concepts.

6. *Extra Practice.* • Have 2 students interview peers or teachers and take notes; after rewriting their notes, ask them to write a summary. • Give credit for keeping study notes about assigned reading; check notebooks on a weekly basis. • In a center, provide notes about a topic currently being studied; have students use the notes to write a summary based upon these and ideas from their textbooks. • Tape 3-minute lectures about topics being studied; have pairs of students listen, take notes, revise, and expand notes; then write a summary. • Adapt ideas from Special Need 35.

37. USING ILLUSTRATIVE AIDS

DETECTION This may be a special skill need of students who:

- Appear confused reading maps
- Have difficulty understanding charts
- Exhibit problems reading graphs
- Do not interpret captions of illustrations
- Ignore most graphic aids

Description. The use of maps, charts, graphs, tables, and pictures is intended to supplement or clarify information presented in textbooks. Illustrative materials are expensive to produce and are not generally used unless the authors and publishers believe further clarification and emphasis are necessary to understand certain portions of the text. However, some students either ignore or misinterpret these learning aids.

Causation. Many students experience difficulty using illustrative material because they have not received regular, direct instruction in how the information can be interpreted and used. Special attention may be given as a lesson on map reading, but map reading is then forgotten until another lesson on map reading appears in the text. Not only the lack of experience but also an inability to transfer concepts from print to graphics can cause students to be confused by the illustrations. Some students are overwhelmed by the clutter of graphics, while others do not read or understand the titles and explanations. Many types of special students experience difficulty interpreting illustrative material.

Implications. To be useful, maps, charts, and graphs should be emphasized each time they are encountered in textbooks. Graphic aids may be used as pre-reading or postreading strategies. As an introductory aid, illustrative information can provide background and an information base from which predictions can be made. As a postreading aid, illustrative material is helpful in expanding concepts, summarizing, or confirming predictions. Graphs and charts are particularly helpful in explaining numerical information. Maps are helpful in showing geographic or territorial boundaries and relative positions of places and routes. Pictures help readers gain a more concrete understanding about topics of study. Pictures and illustrations are also used to add interest and realism to historical and scientific information. As a general study technique, students should be taught to preview all graphics in a chapter before beginning to read the text. The study and application of illustrative aids as they occur in text—instead of occasional map, picture, or graph worksheets—promote their use as intended as well as fosters recognition of their utility and understanding of their contribution to comprehension.

CORRECTION Modify these strategies to meet students' learning needs.

1. *Class Data.* Assist students in making charts and graphs showing the number of students in each class in your school. A table showing height or favorite color might be of interest to the class. Completed chapters or stories can be charted by reading or study groups. Help students make a map of the school using their room as the starting point. Post these illustrative aids for future reference and to use as examples when similar formats appear in textbooks.

2. *Graphic Summaries.* Model the process of converting summary-type information into a graph or chart. Take a chapter summary and use the chalkboard to construct a graph or chart; then discuss how to decide what format to use. Try 2 different formats and then ask your students to decide which format, graph, or table most clearly illustrates the summary information. This strategy works best using scientific or fact-filled text.

3. *Guided Illustrations.* Select information from a textbook. Give students the format and/or categories to use to construct a circle graph (show the circle and divisions in the circle), a table (provide categories), or a map (including the sites or products). Ask students to finish the graphic using the information you provide.

4. *Graphic Switches.* Use simple information containing 4–6 items and present the data as a bar graph. Have your students take the same information in the bar graph and make a circle graph or a chart. The same strategy can be used with textbook aids by having students convert graphic information into another format and then explain how they made the change.

5. *Progress Graphs.* To illustrate the development and utility of graphics, use personal or class graphs to monitor progress in behavior or a subject area. Discuss information as it is added by a class member.

6. *Map Games.* When a particular type of map or several similar maps are used in a textbook, take the opportunity to play Map Games. Historical maps, product maps, weather maps, road maps or other maps can be used as long as they are similar to those presented in a currently used unit of text. Form teams of 2–4 members and take turns asking map-reading questions. If one team misses, the next can try the question. Mix team membership in an effort to give each team members who can keep them in the game. Award at least a first- and second-place winner. Also give credit for the most progress.

7. *Extra Practice.* • Ask students to watch for maps, charts, and graphs in newspapers and magazines; have them bring the graphics to class and explain their meanings to classmates. • Have a weekly contest and ask students to vote for their favorite picture or cartoon caption; then have them practice rewriting the captions. • Have students keep and add to a chart of their grades in 2 subject areas for a reporting period; at the end of the period, have students tape or write an explanation of the chart.

38. USING REFERENCE SOURCES

DETECTION This may be a special skill need of students who:

- Have problems using a table of contents
- Cannot locate words in a dictionary
- Are unable to use textbook indexes
- Cannot use a card catalog
- Have difficulty using encyclopedias
- Are unfamiliar with a thesaurus

Description. In using reference skills, students are involved in two related but different areas: using textbook parts—such as tables of contents, indexes, glossaries, and appendixes—and using reference sources, including dictionaries, encyclopedias, bound indexes, and card catalogs. Neither area receives heavy emphasis, except in certain English classes or from a few teachers who have a special interest in helping students use reference skills. Prerequisite skills include a knowledge of alphabetical order, use of guide words, and the determination of key words for use in locating information.

Causation. Many students who do not use reference skills either have not been sufficiently taught to do so or they do not see the utility of the resources. Some teachers consider the reference skills much like the other study skills as "extras" to be added for the more able students but ignored in favor of the "basics" for low achievers. Other reasons for difficulty include insufficient vocabulary knowledge, inadequate overall reading skills, or incomplete mastery of alphabetical order. Many types of special students, although capable of using references, exhibit this skill need because the bulk of their past instruction has been focused on more obvious skill needs.

Implications. Using book parts represents an assumed area of competence. Students can learn to use the locational aids in their textbooks if they are given sufficient guided instruction and regular opportunities to apply or use the aids. They do not have to master textbook aids before beginning to use auxiliary materials. However, the ability to locate information in textbooks by using an index and a table of contents will make using other reference sources easier. Once resources are explained and guided instruction is provided, frequent applied use of the skills is necessary to build lifelong habits. One problem that must be overcome in teaching the use of dictionaries and other sources of information is often more closely associated with motivation than ability. You may have heard someone say, "It's not that they can't, but they won't." This statement refers to students who see no practical reason to use references.

CORRECTION Modify these strategies to meet students' learning needs.

1. *Using Book Parts.* Emphasize the useful parts of each textbook as you teach from it. Select one particular part of a book that students are reading (e.g., the page numbers, or index, table of contents, or glossary). During 3–4 lessons using the text, incorporate use of the book part with the content lesson. Model and talk students through the use of the chosen skill. Highlight headings and titles as students turn to pages and look for specific information.

2. *Referenced Tests.* Permit students to consult a target reference during tests in several subjects. Tell them ahead of time which reference will be available to them, provide direct instruction in its use, and suggest that they practice using the reference. This strategy often increases motivation to master use of reference and also illustrates their utility.

3. *Detective Teams.* Form 2–3 member detective teams. Take turns asking teams 2-part questions about using reference sources in a textbook. Using a history text, ask, "Where should I look first for the year President Grant took office?" If a team misses, go to the next team still trying for a point. Then follow up with an open team question by asking, "Can you tell us in what year Grant became president?" The first team to find the information gets a point.

4. *Worldly Facts.* A set of encyclopedias will be needed as students are asked to find a specified topic in one of the volumes. Be sure to demonstrate determining which volume to check, using the overall index, and using guide words before having students compete. After students are able to locate information successfully, add a time element. Using teams of 2, name a topic and monitor the amount of time that is necessary to locate it. Save your list of topics and use them again another day. This task can be simplified by having students locate only the volume or by providing the volume and having students locate the topic.

5. *Reference Reports.* Have your students take frequent visits to the library to locate information on a specific topic. Require a written record, telling where they started and each source or reference they checked to find the information. Conference with each student or student team, and help them review their records for accuracy. Finally, have the students explain their steps, sources, and final results to other classmates.

6. *Extra Practice.* • On an independent basis, ask students to use a textbook and make up questions to use for Detective Teams; have them write their questions and answers on index cards. • Have students explain the use of a reference book to a younger student in a lower grade. • Prepare on index cards a group of reference terms to compare and contrast; have pairs of students alternate reading each comparison pair and explaining the similarities and differences (e.g., dictionary/thesaurus, index/table of contents, glossary/index).

REFLECTIONS

1. In Part IV, reading needs are categorized into three general areas: word recognition; comprehension; and study skills. Review the discussion of each of the skills in these areas. Then decide if any skills should be omitted and which additional skills you feel should be discussed. Justify your responses.

2. Part IV notes that study skills are often less emphasized than the other reading skills. Justify this practice. Consider how and when you learned to study. How could your instruction in study skills have been improved? What are the implications for teaching special students?

3. When students read aloud, you hear what they say but do not know what they think; when they read silently, you neither know which words they can pronounce nor what they are thinking. How does this complicate the teacher's task in providing targeted reading instruction? What are the implications for the detection and correction of special oral and silent reading needs?

4. A general overview of reading diagnostic procedures is presented in the introduction to this part of the text. As you review those procedures, consider the types of group-administered reading tests that you have taken. What problems did you experience in responding to the tests? How would your problems compare with those that special students might face? How might these problems affect the validity of the test results?

5. A few of the DETECTION behaviors that signal difficulties with each reading skill are listed at the beginning of each discussion. Observe in a regular and/or a special education classroom to watch for these behaviors. Record any additional behaviors that you observe. Discuss the significance of these behaviors, and ask teachers for their additions to the list.

6. For each special reading need, only a few CORRECTION strategies are listed. Based on your classroom observations and/or your own experience, add to or modify the corrective strategies for the special reading need of your choice.

7. Teaching reading to students with special needs often requires modifying the strategies that are appropriate for teaching most students the same skills. Choose a Special Need from one of those listed in this section. In the teacher's edition of a basal reader, locate the instructional strategies suggested for teaching the same skill. Contrast the teaching activities listed in the teacher's edition with those recommended in this section for that skill. Identify and justify the lesson modifications for students with special needs.

8. Reading lessons can occur either as a separate reading subject or as part of instruction in the other language arts or other subjects. For a special learner, plan two reading lessons: one as a a specific reading lesson and one as a content reading lesson. To design your lessons, use diagnostic information from the school, the materials in use in the school, and the practices and principles in Part I to select and modify your corrective reading strategies.

9. Truly individualized instruction often requires lesson adjustments during teaching. With a peer or a volunteer student, practice the two reading lessons you planned for the special learner. Then actually teach your lessons to the student for whom you planned them, modifying your plans according to the student's responses and needs as you teach.

10. Suggestions for corrective reading instruction for special learners are presented in several reading and special education textbooks. Compare and contrast discussions in these sources with the information in Chapters 9–11:

Alexander, J. E., & Heathington, B. S. (1988). *Assessing and correcting classroom reading problems.* Glenview, IL: Scott, Foresman.

Choate, J. S., & Rakes, T. A. (1989). *Reading: Detecting and correcting special needs.* Boston: Allyn and Bacon.

Ekwall, E. E. (1985). *Locating and correcting reading difficulties* (4th ed.). Columbus, OH: Charles E. Merrill.

Ekwall, E. E., & Shanker, J. L. (1988). *Diagnosis and remediation of the disabled reader* (3rd ed.). Boston: Allyn and Bacon.

Hargis, C. H. (1982). *Teaching reading to handicapped children.* Denver: Love.

Hasenstab, M. S., & Laughton, J. (1982). *Reading, writing, and the exceptional child.* Rockville, MD: Aspen.

Hittleman, D. R. (1988). *Developmental reading K-8: Teaching from a whole-language perspective* (3rd ed.). Columbus, OH: Charles E. Merrill.

Johns, J. L. (1986). *Handbook for remediation of reading difficulties.*Englewood Cliffs, NJ: Prentice-Hall.

McNeil, J. D. (1987). *Reading comprehension: New directions for classroom practice* (2nd ed.). Glenview, IL: Scott, Foresman.

Rupley, W. H., & Blair, T. R. (1988). *Teaching reading: Diagnosis, direct instruction, and practice* (2nd ed.). Columbus, OH: Charles E. Merrill.

Vacca, J. L., Vacca, R. T., & Gove, M. K. (1987). *Reading and learning to read.* Boston: Little, Brown.

Walker, B. J. (1988). *Diagnostic teaching of reading: Techniques for instruction and assessment.* Columbus, OH: Charles E. Merrill.

Wilson, R. M. & Gambrell, L. B. (1988). *Reading comprehension in the elementary school: A teacher's practical guide.* Boston: Allyn and Bacon.

PART V

SPECIAL WRITING NEEDS

Writing is the permanent record of language ideas and is the chief source for evaluating students' knowledge in all subjects. Writing, like speaking, is an encoding or expressive process. As the last in the progressive sequence, it is considered to be the most difficult of the language arts. And the degree of mastery of writing is largely contingent upon the level of achievement of listening, speaking, and reading skills.

The area of writing includes three of the traditional subjects in most elementary curricula: language or English, spelling, and handwriting. The first is a core curricular subject, while the others are the support subjects. At the postelementary levels, the three subjects are generally merged with reading and treated as the single subject of English.

More changes have occurred during the last 10 years in the area of teaching writing than in any other single area of the language arts. Partly as a result of national studies that indicate weak writing skills, the emphasis on writing has increased not only as a subject by itself but also as an important component of instruction in all areas. Writing has evolved from a very mechanical approach to a more integrated and creative process involving all areas of the language arts.

Part V begins with the heart of writing, the expression of ideas in writing, or written expression. While it could be argued that each of the writing skills is a form of written expression, we use the term to differentiate the language and thinking components from the more mechanical facets of writing. Thus, the skills included in Chapter 12 all deal with the process of generating, organizing, and then expressing ideas. These are the skills seldom nurtured and often stifled by teachers who overemphasize mechanics, grammar, spelling, and handwriting.

The mechanics of writing are the topic of Chapter 13, "Written Grammar," and include the traditional skills of capitalization, punctuation, and word usage. Constructing simple and complex sentences is also discussed. In this chapter, the mechanics are treated in a manner that is both practical and timely. It is only in recent years that instruction in written expression has become the process of generating ideas to which grammar and mechanics are applied instead of the more traditional diagramming and parts-of-speech approach. This section concludes with the skill that merges written expression with the mechanics: rewriting, or editing, the final step in the writing process. Thus, mechanics are depicted as a secondary writing function of refining the writing process, applied after the generation and use of ideas and creative expression. This view does not exclude the need for correct writing but instead shifts the emphasis to the content of writing. The sequence of these two chapters is our philosophical statement of their order of importance and the sequence in which they should occur in writing lessons.

The final chapters, 14 and 15, focus on two support subjects: spelling and handwriting. These are not only subjects in which young students are graded but also skills that support and facilitate written expression. Many special learners can memorize the word lists for weekly spelling tests but then cannot remember the correct spellings for use in their daily written assignments. Learning to spell the words that occur frequently in oral and written language simplifies writing tasks. Handwriting is perhaps the most mechanistic of the language arts skills. The way in which students execute their handwriting lessons indicates their understanding of and ability to carefully write correctly. However, since maximum efforts are not always sustained, it is the way in which students write their responses to classroom assignments that reveals the degree of mastery of the handwriting skills. Writing flexibility helps to prevent the handwriting mechanics from interfering with the expression of ideas. The last special need is writing left-handed, a characteristic of a number of special students. This topic is treated separately because instruction for each hand differs.

DETECTION OF SPECIAL WRITING NEEDS

Of the writing skills, perhaps the two that teachers notice most often are the support skills, spelling and handwriting. Of these two skill areas, illegible handwriting probably causes teachers the most grief. Most teachers do not appreciate the daily challenge of deciphering written answers to determine if the content is correct. They can readily tell you who in their class has poor handwriting. Many can also name the poor spellers without consulting the grade book. In contrast, estimates of students' written expression skills or even their written grammar are not usually so obvious.

Formal Detection

While subtests of grammar, mechanics, and spelling are often included in group-administered achievement tests, tests of written expression and handwriting seldom appear. This is primarily because the latter two do not conform to the format of an objective test. Mechanics and grammar are often tested by having students insert or choose the punctuation mark or capital letter that belongs in text or by choosing the label for the part of speech or indicating the words to insert. Spelling is usually tested by having students select the correct word from a choice of four or five spellings. Although such tests do not measure students' abilities to express ideas, the scores sometimes give a rough estimate of a few areas in which individual testing is needed. Very few individually administered formal tests include measures of written language beyond spelling. Those that do usually do not yield enough prescriptive data to plan specific corrective instruction. It is more typically the informal analyses of performance that indicate what to teach.

Informal Detection

The most logical and practical method for informally assessing writing skills is the analysis of students' written work samples. As long as you know the purpose for which an assignment is written, most written samples are appropriate for analysis. It may mean observing students while they write and collecting written work over a period of time, but most elements can be so evaluated. Daily handwriting and spelling are easy to check, particularly if you categorize the students' success and error patterns. Similarly, using a checklist, you can identify from written assignments the specific needs in creative expression, organization, expression of ideas, semantics and syntax, sentence formation, writing mechanics, and the use of different writing forms.

By analyzing written products and observing students as they write, you can often discover significant interfering behaviors, such as the ones cited at the beginning of the discussion of each skill need. Although many students demonstrate some of these key behaviors on occasion, when a pattern of behavior is detected, you may have identified the beginning point for corrective writing instruction.

CORRECTION OF SPECIAL WRITING NEEDS

Writing difficulties are likely to impede students' demonstration of knowledge in all subjects, depending of course on the proportion of written responses and assignments individual teachers make. Handwriting in particular can slow and complicate the recording of ideas. Of the writing skills, written expression is the most difficult because of the sophisticated thinking involved. Although students with intellectual deficits cannot be expected to write ideas beyond the level of their general language functioning, they can be taught to orally express thoughts in their own language for transcription to print and later guided to read and write them. The key idea is to first record the ideas before worrying about the structure and mechanics.

It is important to give students a specific stimulus for writing to help them focus their thoughts and stay on topic. If outlines or concept maps are developed as part of the prewriting process, students have a guide to follow as they write. The recurring theme throughout this section is the need to encourage the expression of ideas and then use the written products to teach the mechanics, grammar, spelling, and even handwriting. The writings may be used as reading material as well. A language experience approach incorporates all the language arts, insures relevance to students' interests and needs, and makes the connections among listening, speaking, reading, and writing. Students with specific spelling problems can be taught how to use resources to locate correct spellings for use in written assignments. Using meaningful content, such as their own compositions, students can be guided to apply punctuation and capitalization. The grammar and rhetoric of a composition can be evaluated and adjusted after the fact by the students themselves. Alternative means of recording responses—such as tape recorders, typewriters, or word processors—are more appropriate than handwriting for some students.

The correction of writing difficulties requires targeted instruction that begins not with writing but with the prerequisite language arts. Providing an experience and then having students first tell about it to a tape recorder for you to transcribe may be the first step. Before deciding upon specific CORRECTION strategies, particularly for identified special learners, consult the practices and principles in Part I and the opening discussion for each of the other language arts—listening, speaking, and reading. Once you select strategies, modify them according to students' individual learning needs.

39. GETTING STARTED

DETECTION This may be a special skill need of students who:

- Are hesitant to begin writing
- Would rather copy than generate language
- Have difficulty staying on the topic
- Are unable to write more than a few sentences
- Dislike writing

Description. Written expression is, for most students, clearly an outgrowth of oral language activity. The development of sentence sense and basic sentence patterns is typically established before the age of six. Although some students experience language acquisition delays, steps taken to bring about improvement in oral language typically improve written expression as well. The "getting started" step is probably the most important one for building written expression skills, expressing ideas, and maintaining interest in writing.

Causation. Beginning to write usually occurs out of curiosity, need, or teacher assignment. Some teachers' forced, tightly structured "my way" instruction simply turns students off to writing. Teachers who dwell on the mechanics of writing rather than the expression of ideas also inhibit young writers. Problems associated with poor vision, hearing, or use of fine-motor skills can complicate the process. Language problems and communications disorders also affect writing as well as other language-generation functions.

Implications. In the beginning stages of written expression, it is particularly important to all but ignore the mechanics of writing, focusing instead on the content of the ideas expressed. Later, the students' writing can be used to teach the application of mechanics. Learning to write means having students write frequently. At the same time, frequent writing assignments are of little value if they are not varied, interesting, and audience directed. You will notice repeated references to process writing, stressing that the process is more important than the product. The generation of written language involves a three-step sequence: prewriting, composing, and revising or editing. It is through guided practice during each of these phases that students actually learn to write. Inferred within the process is the idea that planning and editing are just as important as composing. Each of the three steps makes an important contribution to the improvement of written products.

CORRECTION Modify these strategies to meet students' learning needs.

1. *Group Stories.* Experience charts, dictated stories, or Group Stories all involve students in contributing ideas to form sentences of a story as someone prints or writes their statements on the chalkboard or transparency. Use a common experience or activity to stimulate language and then solicit contributions from as many different students as possible. Reproduce the students' stories as close to their spoken dictation as possible. Have them read the story with you several times, and then copy the story with the title they agree upon. Save the story for later use to involve students in proofreading and rewriting, or proofwriting. Emphasize generating and using language to express ideas, not producing publishable stories.

2. *Idea Banks.* Provide a table, file box or bulletin board for displaying or filing "Ideas for Authors." Encourage students to contribute pictures or titles of favorite topics as well as those teacher-selected topics featured in weekly lessons. To save as a reference, select 1–2 students to record on cards good ideas that students have used during a particular week. Feature "Picks of the Week" writing on a bulletin board.

3. *Story Openers.* Story Openers are nothing more than sharp words to stimulate students' imaginations or memories as they begin a writing project. Guide students until they feel comfortable. Instead of suggesting an opener, try to give at least 2–3 choices. Self-selection generally improves the quality and ease of generation of written work. After finishing a lesson on weather, for example, these Story Openers could be used: "My favorite kind of day . . .," "After the thunder we. . .," or "Showers of sunlight . . ." These are sentence starters; topics can be suggested as students progress.

4. *Questions.* Using a Story Opener or a topic, talk students through the process of asking questions about a topic. Then guide them to compose by writing the answers to their questions.

5. *Post and Praise.* Emphasize effort more than product. Encourage and build pride in early written efforts. Overemphasis on detail can limit joy and creativity. After displaying work for at least a week, call an editors' conference to proofwrite the compositions as a group before reposting.

6. *Extra Practice.* • Ask students to bring topics from home or TV to write about. • Have students work in groups to construct Story Openers for younger students or classmates. • Have students select the best opening sentences from their texts and use them as story starters. • Adapt strategies from Special Needs 12 and 13.

40. USING DIFFERENT FORMS

DETECTION This may be a special skill need of students who:

- Cannot write paragraphs
- Do not understand the concept of story writing
- Are unable to write descriptively
- Exhibit problems writing letters
- Hesitate to write short notes or captions
- Have difficulty generating initial ideas for writing (SN 39)

Description. Part of the growth process associated with written expression includes learning to express ideas in many different forms. Forms of writing can include a variety of letters, notes, compliments, acceptances, essays, stories, and an assortment of descriptive or personal paragraphs and compositions. The major forms generally required by the classroom curriculum are the utilitarian ones that follow a structured format. The more creative forms, such as poetry and plays, are naturally less structured and are discussed as Special Need 42.

Causation. The greatest restrictions on students' use of different writing forms result from a lack of proper guidance, stimulation, feedback, and modeling by teachers. Most students need specific types of strategies that engage them in a process they can understand and complete within a reasonable amount of time. As in nearly all writing, physical or psychological handicaps interfere with the process. However, these highly structured formats are more readily mastered than are the primarily creative forms.

Implications. Teachers usually select those forms of writing that they enjoy most and concentrate their instruction accordingly. It is important to share many forms of writing with students and be careful not to overemphasize the favorite types. Give students extra opportunities with their preferred forms of writing instead of stressing yours. Once students learn to enjoy writing with confidence, you can be more directive. Older students in particular need instruction that focuses on real-life writing demands, such as completing applications. Considerable modeling and talk-through is needed to teach the various forms of written expression. Writing an answer to a question is very different from writing a letter of inquiry or a book review. Each type of expression must be modeled and accompanied by visual examples that are left available for continued reference. In addition to writing every day, students should have some choices in the selection of topics, and the audience to whom the writing is addressed should be varied.

CORRECTION Modify these strategies to meet students' learning needs.

1. *Letter Lessons.* Letter writing is one of the most useful and motivating writing experiences available. As an extension of letter writing, capitalization, punctuation, and sentence-writing skills can be integrated into the proofwriting process. Every letter should have a purpose. Begin by modeling a simple letter on the board, and have students take turns suggesting what they would like to say. Leave the model visible and circulate as students write a personal letter to someone. For example:

    Dear Mom,   Dear Dad,

    I love you.   OR   Come to PTO tonight.

    Love,   Love,
    Sandy   Tommy

    As students progress, begin to expand the contents of the letters by providing sentence and paragraph starters for students to finish. Provide opportunities for students to mail or deliver their letters.
2. *Special Delivery.* Have students write letters about themselves and share them with each other or with students in another class. Have the letters delivered, and arrange for responses to be written by the recipients. Permit note writing in class if and only if the notes conform to your posted form for informal letters.
3. *Nice Notes.* Inform students about the occasions when thank you, acceptance, reminder, and other types of notes are important. Demonstrate what information is used in each type of note, and post several samples; then provide a situation each day that calls for writing a note. Be sure to include note writing for birthdays, surprises, holidays, and notices to parents.
4. *Creative Captions.* Using videotapes of popular TV shows, turn off the sound and then pause selected scenes; have students write captions to fit the scenes. Or have students write captions for pictures and cartoons; display selected creative captions.
5. *Story Segments.* Provide portions of oral or written stories, and have students write the story endings or beginnings. Model the process, and then write a few sample beginnings and endings. Use this technique to extend reading lessons instead of always asking questions.
6. *Dear Editor.* Help students write and publish a class newspaper. Include a column for letters to the editor. For the first edition, you should be the editor as a model; thereafter, have the class select a different editor for each edition. Assign each student a different role for each edition.
7. *Extra Practice.* • Use groups of students to construct special letters of inquiry, thank you, or invitation to companies or people in the community. • Provide stories or paragraphs with 2–3 sentences deleted in the middle of the text; have students add the missing information so that it makes sense according to the rest of the material. • Ask students to write notes to remind peers about assignments or important items to bring to class.

41. ORGANIZING AND REPORTING INFORMATION

DETECTION This may be a special skill need of students who:

- Have trouble selecting a specific topic for writing
- Cannot complete forms and applications
- Have difficulty staying on the topic
- Cannot gather and organize data
- Are generally disorganized in completing assignments
- Often omit important details in written work
- Also have problems making oral presentations (SN 15)

Description. Among the formats for written reporting are formal class reports, announcements, advertisements, commercials, and stories. Special types of reporting include writing the appropriate information on various forms and applications and writing an autobiography or resumé. The writing must be directed to both the intended audience and the purpose or use of information. Reporting can be used to sell an idea, product, or service or even oneself. The length of school reports can vary from a few sentences to hundreds of sentences, depending on the purpose of the report, the intended audience, and the students' writing abilities.

Causation. A lack of familiarity and practice causes some students to have problems writing reports. The primary reasons for students' inability to write reports are much the same as those cited for difficulties expressing ideas in other forms, Special Need 40: a lack of modeling, stimulation, proper guidance, and feedback. Insufficient mastery of prerequisite writing skills, vocabulary knowledge, presentation skills, and reading skills, as well as the study skills needed for writing summaries and taking notes, also interferes with performance. Poor organization and lack of focus inhibit students' abilities to narrow a topic and then stick to it. Special students who may experience difficulty writing reports include the culturally and language different, behavior disordered, language disabled, learning disabled, and mentally retarded.

Implications. Report writing, unlike story writing, is often less creative and includes more information gathering, expanding, and combining of information into an organized written format. Even though mastery of study skills facilitates report writing, instruction in the two areas can occur concurrently, with an emphasis on summary writing. Correction should begin with short, interesting reporting formats and move toward the more lengthy class project reports. Short writing activities (e.g., announcements or news spots) can be motivational. Written debates about controversial issues help students focus and stay on the topic. Important to all students but especially older students is guidance to collect and organize data and then insert the information on various forms and applications.

CORRECTION Modify these strategies to meet students' learning needs.

1. *ID Cards.* For real-world reporting, guide students to collect and then write on an index card important identifying information about themselves. Include personal and emergency information and, for older students, references, school and job history, and the like. Photo-reduce the card for students to keep. Guide students to transfer the data from the card to real forms (e.g., library card, office record card, or applications for jobs, insurance, driver's license). Later, use the cards to begin writing an autobiography or resumé.

2. *Outline Reporting.* Teach outlining as a tool for reporting. For the major topics, list the reporter questions: who, what, where, when, how, and why. Read aloud a news article and have students write the answers to these questions. Then guide them to add subordinate details. Finally, have them use their outlines to write the reports. After several guided experiences, have students choose a topic from audiotapes or books to outline report.

3. *Systems.* Teach a system for writing a report. One simple system includes these steps: a) select a topic, b) gather references and take notes, c) organize subtopics and notes using a map or outline, d) write a draft of the report, and e) proofread and revise copy. Note that this plan parallels a process-writing approach. Each stage is important, requiring guidance, demonstration, clarification, and monitoring. Walk students through several contributed reports before they begin independent or team efforts.

4. *Minireports.* Help students write brief reports—such as announcements, short commercials for good books, past events, or trips—to place at a reading center or post on an information board. Provide students with the sources needed for the report. Initially, concentrate on outlining or mapping by deciding what needs to be said. Next, actually write and then proofwrite. Narrowing topics and gathering information can be added to the system as students progress. Provide a standard reporting format until students feel a need to expand their coverage. Include such units as these: What, When, Where, Who, and sometimes Results.

5. *Packaged Reports.* Present several sources of data, such as a part of a story, related news clipping, and notes from a book. Guide students to turn the data into a short report by deciding on a topic, organizing, draftwriting, and proofwriting. Have additional references available.

6. *Parallel Reports.* Give students a structured format to write brief reports to supplement science or history topics. Provide several different science or history textbooks so that students can concentrate on using the information, not hunting for sources. Later, have students use locational and reference sources to write their reports.

7. *Extra Practice.* • Have students keep daily journals to practice reporting. • Have students identify information sources for news reports, list them, and share them with the class. • Ask students to contribute information for class reports to parents. • Adapt ideas from Special Needs 15 and 20.

42. WRITING CREATIVELY

DETECTION This may be a special skill need of students who:

- Have difficulty responding spontaneously
- Write best using facts and information sources
- Are reluctant to write stories
- Attend to mechanics more than content
- Appear anxious writing about personal or original ideas

Description.   Creative writing is the written expression of personal ideas, experiences, and interpretations. Many students enjoy writing stories, poems, plays, and jingles. In fact, the more students enjoy writing, the more likely they are to write and improve their written expression. Once a pattern of consistent production, confidence, and interest has been established, targeted skills can be developed using the students' own writing. Unfortunately, some teachers believe that targeted skill instruction is more important than imaginative, less structured writing experiences.

Causation.   The attitudes and philosophies of teachers disable many would-be creative writers. When teachers place more emphasis on correctness than on expression of ideas or praise the traditional and shun the novel, students soon learn to write the teacher's thoughts, not their own ideas. Many teachers use a single, structured writing assignment to grade students on their creative expression, form, grammar, spelling, and handwriting, thereby presenting students with a stressful, uncreative, and almost impossible task. Some youngsters feel they are not creative and have little to say. Most students, however, even special students, can write creatively when encouraged to do so without fear of failure, freed of the writing mechanics, and assured that it is permissible to express what they think in their own words.

Implications.   Students must know that they can express their ideas, free from censure. Creative writing experiences should be just that, not grammar or mechanics lessons. The students' writings, once freely expressed, are the most logical, personal, and relevant source of materials for follow-up editorial lessons in grammar and mechanics. Therefore, it is imperative that the grading of the content be separated from the grading of the grammar. To stimulate creative expression, three conditions are necessary: 1) the appropriate environment, including plenty of resources and references, a center as a place to write and find ideas, and a classroom attitude conveying a supportive, nonthreatening approach to written efforts; 2) the provision of numerous experiences and strategies to stimulate creative writing of all types and in all lessons; 3) and teachers who provide an audience, guided modeling, and regular conferences. In many instances, creativity will need to be tapped orally first and then in writing.

CORRECTION Modify these strategies to meet students' learning needs.

1. *Idea Generators.* As students routinely share, question, and participate in classroom experiences, watch for clues to areas of interest or excitement. Keep a list of these high-interest topics at the writing center. A few topics many students like to write about include characters in stories and books, favorite singers, sports and super heroes, animals, Indians, space, inventions, fashion, self-improvement, music, and hobbies.
2. *Special Poetry.* Directions for teaching the writing of poetry are included in most writing programs. You may be familiar with free verse, alternate-line rhyming, cinquain, haiku, and senryu formats. The two formats in which students are not required to use rhyme— acrostic and diamontic— offer ample opportunity to express personal ideas and are appropriate for almost any interest or ability level.

ACROSTIC FORMAT

Puppy and me	Cooking is my heart's delight.
Like to run. He's	Ovens and recipes
Always happy and	Overrun our
Yelping for more.	Kitchen and my tummy.

DIAMONTIC FORMAT

Winter	Sad
Cold, Wet	Down, Lost
Dark, Bright, Sun	Blue, Cheerful, Singing
Swimming, Hot	Bubbling, Playful
Summer	Happy

3. *Conferencing.* Use individual writing conferences as an integral part of the writing program. Hold regular conferences for 3–5 minutes to discuss on-going writing efforts. These guidelines may be helpful in conducting conferences: a) Go to the students at their desks; b) Attempt to have the students do at least half the talking; c) Take notes about what you discuss; this shows your interest and provides a written record; and d) Ask students to retell what was discussed and summarize with them.
4. *Simulations.* Describe simulated or hypothetical situations as writing starters. For example, after reading a story, have students interject themselves into the story and write how their lives change and how the story changes; have them project themselves into some future or past time and write about their experiences; or describe a change in their current environment and have them react in writing. The possibilities are limitless as long as the enthusiasm is high.
5. *Extra Practice.* • Bind creative writings; have students read and/or edit the writings of peers. • Have students change and rewrite taped stories. • Have students write daily in a creative writing journal. • Adapt strategies from Special Needs 17 and 20.

43. WRITING SENTENCES

DETECTION This may be a special skill need of students who:

- Frequently write incomplete or run-on sentences
- Respond orally with incomplete or run-on sentences
- Converse in incomplete sentences
- Frequently start over when writing

Description. Written sentence construction is largely based upon students' habitual use of complete sentences in oral language. The task also requires students to think in complete idea units and have command of a reasonable vocabulary and the handwriting skills to record the oral language as written language. The handwriting component involves the more mechanical aspects discussed as Special Needs 52–55. Teaching sentence production usually begins from an oral base and progresses somewhat sequentially. Beginning writers do not have to know the definition of a sentence in order to speak and write in complete sentences. They do, however, need a working knowledge or feel for both semantics, the meaning of the words, and syntax, the logical order of the words within sentences.

Causation. Sentence writing can be limited by any number of language or communications disorders, ranging from delayed language development to more serious pathologically based speech and language disorders. The oral language of students who have had little exposure to rich, fluent spoken language often reflects that limited language background. Students who speak in single words or phrases are not likely to write in complete sentences. If these same students also have had little experience using written language, you can expect their sentence production to be unsatisfactory.

Implications. Manuscript, cursive, keyboard, or other alternative writing formats can be used for the mechanical renderings of sentence construction. As students begin to generate oral phrasing and sentence statements, you may need to first write the statements for students to copy. Since both are mutually reinforcing, written language intervention should occur concurrently with oral language sentencing. An integrated language-based approach—combining listening, speaking, reading, and writing—should be used.

CORRECTION Modify these strategies to meet students' learning needs.

1. *Oral Sentences.* Model complete sentences when you speak, and whenever possible, require students to initiate and respond in complete sentences. To avoid the trap of teaching students to speak in single words or phrases as they answer your oral questions, tell them to "Pretend I didn't ask a question." Have them answer questions in complete sentences much as though they are initiating a conversation with the statement of a fact or opinion.

2. *Sentence Builders.* Print on the board introductory phrases from sentences related to a topic or story currently being studied in class. Have students supply the ending part of each sentence. Read aloud the sentence openers and ask students to orally finish each sentence based on what they recall from the lesson. As each answer is given, write it on the board and then have the student read the entire sentence aloud. Then, give students the sentence openers on the board, and also list the words that might be needed to finish them. Have students copy the opening part and finish each sentence in writing. Vary the procedure by supplying the sentence endings; have students supply the sentence openers and write each complete sentence.

3. *Too Much Sentence.* Guide students to compose sentences from groups of words. Begin by giving them sentences with 1–2 extra words inserted. Read or have students read aloud each sentence to decide which words to cross out (e.g., "The dog sat ran the fast"). Model the thinking process for deciding which words do not belong. Have students practice; then present groups of scrambled words for students to rearrange into sentences. Finally, give students scrambled word groups but with too many words in each group; have them choose the words and then rearrange them into sentences.

4. *Sentence Parts.* Underline or circle the 2 basic parts of a sentence, explaining that one is the telling part and one is the doing part, or the subject and predicate. Guide students to mark sentences accordingly. Use these markings to highlight basic sentence patterns. Have students contribute their words and topics to build simple sentences.

5. *Word Changes.* After completing a lesson, use the same text on transparencies to play Word Changes. Divide the class into 2 teams. Have the first team point to a word in a sentence. The other team must suggest a different but appropriate word to replace the target word, and then write the new sentence on the board. If a team cannot suggest a word, the other team gets the turn. Continue play until neither team can suggest further changes. Most of the text should have been rewritten with little or no meaning change. Pairs of students can also play the game.

6. *Extra Practice.* • Using consumable text, have students underline the beginning and end of each sentence in a paragraph, and then write a sentence of their own that would fit into the story. • Use a modified cloze format to encourage sentence building. • Tape sentence openers or endings, and have students tape their responses to Sentence Builders. • Adapt ideas from Special Need 44.

44. COMBINING AND EXPANDING SENTENCES

DETECTION This may be a special skill need of students who:

- Frequently use short sentences
- Use run-on sentences
- Tend to write excessively long sentences
- Often use incomplete sentences (SN 43)
- Have difficulty editing written work (SN 48)

Description. Sentence writing represents a key ingredient in developing students' writing skills. Early writing is often filled with excessive use of the words *said, and, or,* and *but* to join sentences. There is reason to expect that direct instruction in combining and expanding sentences will improve students' writing. Sometimes referred to as *sentence reconstruction, editing,* or *rewriting,* combining sentences involves joining two or more sentences into one meaningful sentence. Expansion refers to expanding one or more sentences into two or more meaningful sentences.

Causation. Poor reading or listening comprehension, an underdeveloped writing vocabulary, and lack of writing experience can limit students' efforts in combining and expanding sentences. Students who have difficulty generating sentences, Special Need 40, are also likely to have similar problems combining and expanding them. Students who habitually speak in phrases or short sentences, who are from culturally or language-different backgrounds, or who exhibit general language difficulties may have special problems combining and expanding.

Implications. The combining and expanding of sentences is an important step toward building and improving skills in written expression. Knowing the parts of speech or being able to use long words is not enough to produce coherent, scholarly writing. Sentence building is necessary in order to produce paragraphs and ultimately longer written works. Comprehension is a major contributor to the ability to combine or expand ideas and words. As in the case of most writing experiences, the use of sentence-building strategies is most effective when provided in conjunction with other subject-area lessons. Guided practice is often necessary to model how to develop and rearrange sentences. This practice can easily be presented as a part of a history, reading, or science lesson. In addition to helping students to improve their writing skills, such presentations also reinforce knowledge of the particular subject area. Every student should be involved in a writing experience at the appropriate level every school day. Combining and expanding can be a part of a planned writing experience, whether it is directed toward composition, reporting, note-taking, or story writing.

CORRECTION Modify these strategies to meet students' learning needs.

1. *Grow-Up Sentences.* Say 2–3 short, choppy sentences. Have students restate them to sound more like "older students" or adults. Begin with very obvious examples such as "I came. I ate. I slept." The sentences may be either combined or expanded to sound more mature. Then use examples from the beginning of the preprimer book of the students' reading series or, better yet, from an old preprimer; have students restate the sentences to sound like the text of their current reading level. After restating the sentences, have students write them.

2. *Visual Models.* Using examples from students' textbooks, provide visual models (e.g., posters, folders, samples of student work) to reflect a specific example of writing. A sample model for sentence expansion or combining that also stresses the accompanying punctuation is:

> We were ready to go.
>
> }   We were ready, but no one showed up.
>
> No one showed up.
>
> The team was good.
>
> }   The team was good, so they won the game.
>
> They won the game.

Using this same format, present sentence pairs for students to complete. For students who produce excessively long sentences, a similar format can be used to shorten sentences:

> Our trip was long and we became   1.   *Space provided*
> tired and hungry before it   }   *for rewrites*
> was over and we made it home.   2.   *here.*
>   (Given to students)

3. *Sentence Assembly.* Provide sentences written on sentence strips or tagboard. Have students move the strips (2–3 per sentence) around to make good sentences; discuss and evaluate the new sentences.

4. *Jumbled Sentences.* Take 3–6 sentences from a current textbook and print the words on cards. Include as extra words the ones your students overuse or fail to use. Have students construct sentences and compare their sentences with those in the text.

5. *Team Interchange.* Form teams and orally give students 1 long or several short sentences. To score a point, a team has 1–2 minutes to come up with an appropriate sentence orally or in writing. Other teams may work at the same time to be ready if the first team fails.

6. *Extra Practice.* • Try the above ideas using sentence transformations instead. \• Appoint student editors to review class work and make suggestions for combining or expanding ideas. • Have students rewrite paragraphs by expanding, combining, or reducing sentences. • Adapt strategies from Special Needs 43 and 48.

45. USING PARTS OF SPEECH

DETECTION This may be a special skill need of students who:

- Frequently use nouns and verbs that do not agree
- Confuse word choices when writing
- Misuse structure words
- Cannot identify major parts of speech
- Have generally weak language skills
- Exhibit usage problems in oral language (SN 13)

Description. The major parts of speech that must be mastered for fluent writing include nouns, pronouns, verbs, adjectives, and adverbs. Making appropriate word choices and using structure words are also important. Function words include using noun markers, verb markers, negatives, and question markers. Although several categories of structure words exist, mastery of the major ones is generally the main concern of students who have difficulty. Other categories, including qualifiers and prepositions, should be introduced, explained, and used as student writing requires.

Causation. Written word usage is typically a direct reflection of oral word usage and thus of students' habitual language patterns. Students from culturally or language-different backgrounds and those who experience general language difficulties may have significant problems with correct word usage, even after intensive instruction. Problems are also created by failure to recognize the real-life relevance of parts of speech and by the the fear and dread many students have of writing. Inconsistent instruction is responsible for some usage difficulties. Not all teachers have made the complete transition from the grammatical teachings of their own school days to the newer linguistic orientations, retaining some of the "old school" beliefs emphasizing recognition level categorizing, identifying, and correct usage. The result is a mixture of instruction. If students are not interested, academically delayed, or confused by a varied background, more generative types of instructional procedures are appropriate.

Implications. The teaching of grammar and the parts of speech in particular has changed since the 1960s. Diagramming and phrasing activities are no longer considered particularly useful. Although some teachers still use the traditional ordering of sentence parts, the newer linguistic-based strategies approach teaching the parts of speech as a more active, usage-based experience. A dependence upon student-generated language instead of recognition is recommended. Strategies that include actual manipulation of language as a function of the writing process are preferred over more restrictive charting models of teaching.

CORRECTION Modify these strategies to meet students' learning needs.

1. *Living Sentences.* Use sentence strips to print 2–3 parts of a sentence on paper. Give individual students a part of the sentence and ask them to look at their part as well as their classmates' and stand in order to make a sentence. After the sentence is completed, have a student write it on the board. Discuss the parts of speech in each sentence that are appropriate for the students' level. Label the parts of speech above the sample words; ask for additional examples. Capitalization and punctuation can also be emphasized, if appropriate.

2. *Read-Aloud Cloze.* Using a reading or content text, read aloud a passage, but delete all the words in a particular category, such as adverbs. Have the students supply the missing words based on the context and their past experiences with the particular passage. Then, identify and discuss the particular part of speech and the function of the missing words in each sentence. As new parts of speech are presented, use the same passages but delete all the words in the new category. For practice, have students work in pairs using passages that you supply.

3. *Writers' Cloze.* An entertaining and motivational way to teach parts of speech is to follow the format of *Mad Libs*, the consumable pads of cloze activities available from Price, Stern, and Sloan Publishers. Use a passage from a reading or content text as in the above activity. Delete every word of a certain category, but before reading aloud the passage, have students suggest, for example, 5 adjectives (or describing words). Then, read the passage with the suggested words inserted. The resulting stories are usually quite humorous. For practice, construct additional similar stories for pairs of students to complete or present selections from *MAD LIBS*.

4. *Sentence Frames.* After explaining, identifying, and using nouns and/or verbs in sentences, solicit student sentences; guide students to locate nouns and verbs. Write sentence frames on the board, omitting nouns, verbs, or both. Model the process of filling in the frames. Then have students complete sentences on their own, write them on the board, and discuss them.

5. *Personalized Intervention.* One of the best methods of dealing with parts of speech is to use students' written work and direct specific follow-up intervention addressing the problems in their writing. Special lessons can be presented individually or in small groups of students with similar problems. After the lesson, have your students revise their own work according to what they have just learned.

6. *Extra Practice.* • After a subject-area lesson, have pairs of students take turns pointing to structure words or parts of speech in their text and having classmates identify them. • Have an editor's table in class where students can read other students' papers to find examples of specified usage. • Have students compose sentences using a posted list of words in each category and a formula you supply (e.g., noun + verb + adverb). • Adapt strategies from Special Needs 11, 13, and 18.

46. PUNCTUATING CORRECTLY

DETECTION This may be a special skill need of students who:

- Fail to use punctuation
- Use punctuation incorrectly
- Do not recognize the function of specific punctuation marks
- Exhibit poor phrasing during oral reading (SN 28)
- Do not capitalize correctly (SN 47)

Description. Used as markers to convey meaning, punctuation provides signals to assist readers to understand written material and writers to express their thoughts as they would speak them. Some experts consider the use of punctuation marks to be similar in function to the use of nonverbal gestures, facial expressions, and voice intonation in oral speech. The punctuation marks that are the most basic are periods, question marks, commas, and quotation marks. Other punctuation marks should be introduced and used as needed.

Causation. Isolated practice without sufficient application across the curriculum causes some students to see punctuation as just another meaningless detail, like capitalization. Ineffective instruction is a major contributor to skill deficiencies; however, when presented as a code to oral language, even students with general language deficits can master punctuation if they speak with expression. Students who do not observe punctuation when reading orally may have particular difficulty learning to punctuate when writing. Because hearing losses may interfere with recognition of intonation, expression, and phrasing, hearing-impaired students may experience some problems mastering punctuation. Those gifted students who tend to overlook details may not punctuate with consistent accuracy. Many students with special needs are capable of mastering punctuation because it is one of the more mechanical aspects of written expression.

Implications. To be successful, most students need an approach that integrates oral experiences and demonstrations using proper intonation, teacher modeling using student work on the chalkboard, and structured practice requiring students to insert punctuation into text. Continuous guided practice for using particular types of punctuation is also needed. Impromptu instruction can occur when sentences are written on the board by simply pausing for students to suggest the correct punctuation. Students tend to learn more effectively when the use of punctuation is explained, applied, and presented as a participatory experience in all subjects as a natural part of the writing process. After students have expressed their ideas in writing, have them proofwrite for punctuation. Mastery results from regular use in daily writing for both personal and academic purposes.

CORRECTION Modify these strategies to meet students' learning needs.

1. *Integrated Punctuation.* Present on transparencies groups of 3–4 sentences from easy reading lessons that illustrate only the target punctuation marks; highlight the punctuation marks. Have students chorally read to observe and emphasize punctuation. Next, give students copies of the sentences but without punctuation; have them read aloud each sentence with you and then insert the correct punctuation.

2. *Spotlight Punctuation.* As different punctuation marks are presented, add them to a poster that can serve as a class reference. To spotlight the relevance of punctuation, use sentence strips with student sentences, showing an example of each target mark. Change examples regularly to reflect samples from actual lessons. A sample poster might read:

   - A PERIOD IS USED FOR INITIALS, TITLES, AND TO END STATEMENTS.
     Mr. Tim K. Jackson was Susie's teacher.
   , A COMMA IS USED IN DATES AND AFTER ITEMS IN A SERIES.
     Jim's birthday is October 11, 1981.
     They grow corn, wheat, and beans.

3. *Punctuation Explanation.* Copy from a textbook onto a transparency a selection that students have already read and discussed. Then, referring to posted guidelines for punctuation, help students explain the reason for punctuation marks. Have them repeat the procedure using several selections from their textbooks.

4. *Punctuation Error.* Retype passages that are familiar to the students, but delete the punctuation or punctuate incorrectly. List at the top of the page the number of punctuation errors. Have students find the errors, correct them, and then decide why someone might make each particular error. Using transparencies, model the process; then discuss common errors.

5. *Oral Punctuation.* Read a passage to the class; pause and reread certain statements. Have students decide which punctuation mark(s) is needed. If stories from a textbook are used, have students verify their responses in their books. Then give students consumable copies of each passage but without the punctuation; have them insert punctuation as they read aloud.

6. *Punctuation Board.* Using a flannelboard or sentence chart that holds sentence strips or punctuation-mark cards, write student-dictated sentences on sentence strips. Have small groups or teams of students insert the proper punctuation in the sentences. Capitalization can also be added by providing upper-case letters on cards. Use sentences from content lessons to reinforce new content and apply punctuation in a meaningful context.

7. *Extra Practice.* • Ask students to look for punctuation in magazines, circle each mark, and explain its function. • End each day by having pairs of students exchange dictated sentences to punctuate. • Have young students develop names for punctuation marks, such as Paula Period, Comma Connie, Donnie Dash, and Question Mark Mary. • Adapt ideas from Special Need 47.

47. CAPITALIZING APPROPRIATELY

DETECTION This may be a special skill need of students who:

- Often omit capitalization
- Use too many capital letters
- Capitalize at random
- Correctly capitalize only certain types of words
- Do not punctuate correctly (SN 46)

Description. Capitalization involves the use of capital letters to signal meaning or respect in written material. The capital letters themselves convey meaning in that they clarify the intent and use of certain words and terms. Although not intended to be memorized and recited, a few basic guidelines for capitalization are pertinent: 1) Capitalize your first and last name; 2) Capitalize the word *I*; 3) Capitalize the first word in a sentence; 4) Capitalize personal titles like Ms., Mr., and Mrs.; 5) Capitalize place names; and 6) Capitalize days, holidays, and months. These guidelines should be posted in the classroom, but to be valuable, they should be applied daily in writing.

Causation. Lack of familiarity with capitalization is a problem for many students. The two major reasons for problems mastering this skill are ineffective instruction and language problems that interfere with students' understanding of the actual categories of words to be capitalized. The first situation can be easily remedied with appropriate corrective instruction. The second cause is more difficult to correct because it involves a conceptual weakness and often a general language deficit, such as that exhibited by some students who are culturally or language different, hearing impaired, language disabled, or mentally retarded. A few gifted students may capitalize incorrectly, not because they do not understand the rules or language but because they are not concerned with details.

Implications. Capitalization is generally easier for most students to master than is punctuation. Both skills are usually taught together because they involve similar instructional materials and related concepts. With the proper instruction, students who understand the language categories of the words to be capitalized can typically master capitalization with relative ease. It is important to use as a source of instructional material the personal experiences and writings of students, including their names, familiar places, and characters. Initial instruction should be targeted toward one or two of the categories of words. Once instruction has begun, you may find that the overuse of capitalization is a greater problem than underuse, a point at which to review the posted guidelines. Have students check the capitalization of original compositions after they have expressed their ideas. Proofwriting increases the probability of correct capitalization in future compositions.

CORRECTION Modify these strategies to meet students' learning needs.

1. *Student Directory.* Ask students to contribute to a class directory. Include information such as full name, address, title of favorite movie or book, and the names of any pets or favorite animals. Have peers check each entry to be sure that capital letters are used correctly. Reproduce the directory so each student can have a personal copy.

2. *Big or Small.* Using words on index cards, show students names of classmates, cities, or other words that are usually capitalized. Mix in a few words that should not be capitalized. Organize 2 teams and have them take turns stating "big" or "small," depending on whether the word should be capitalized or not, referring to the posted guidelines to prove their answers. Follow this isolated recognition with an immediate application of capitalization, using as many of the same words as possible in context.

3. *Capital Explanation.* Copy from a textbook onto a transparency a selection that students have already read and discussed. Then, referring to the posted guidelines for capitalization, guide students to explain why each word in the selection is capitalized. Have them locate in their textbooks several other selections and follow a similar procedure, explaining and discussing each instance of capitalization. Then as an independent activity, give students a consumable passage to explain. Have them refer to the posted guidelines for the number of each category that explains each capital letter in the selection and then write that correct number beside each capital letter.

4. *Capital Error.* Retype passages that are familiar to the students, but add or delete several capital letters. List at the top of the page the number (but not the type) of capitalization errors. Have students find the errors, correct them, and then decide why someone might make each particular error. Using transparencies, model the process; then discuss common errors.

5. *Personality Caps.* Provide a careful explanation and illustration of proper capitalization for letter writing. Next, solicit student input for a group letter to a favorite cartoon character, sports personality, or singer; write the letter on the chalkboard without using any capitalization. Ask students to help add proper capitalization. Leave the proper letter on the board. Then have students work in small groups or independently to either construct their own letter or capitalize words in a second letter you provide. Circulate as students work, and provide guidance as needed.

6. *Extra Practice.* • Ask students to underline or circle all the capitalized words in a passage; then have a peer explain why each word is capitalized. • As a matter of practice, have students proofread another student's written work for proper capitalization. • Have students develop a list of words they frequently fail to capitalize or needlessly capitalize and the reason each should be capitalized; then have them use their list to proofread their own written work before turning it in.

48. REVISING

DETECTION This may be a special skill need of students who:

- Do not correct careless errors in written assignments
- Do not revise their assignments to improve them
- Seldom use vivid and descriptive language
- Use poor grammar and sentence structure (SN 43–45)
- Do not check work for spelling and organization (SN 50–51)
- Use inappropriate punctuation or capitalization (SN 46–47)
- Turn in illegible written assignments (SN 53–55)

Description.   Revising is the third major step in the writing process, following prewriting and composing. Editing or revising written language involves proofreading to identify elements to correct or to improve. The rewriting process includes proofwriting to reword, organize, or clarify content, making changes in grammar, spelling, and punctuation and improving the legibility of the handwriting or typing and the overall appearance. In this final polishing step, students pull together several language skills and apply them to a written product.

Causation.   Many students are not familiar with the final stage of writing. Still others lack several of the enabling skills that are needed to express ideas, improve wording, or spot misspellings. Even students who have mastered the skills may not take or have the time to edit. Those who work slowly, wait until the last minute, or are in a hurry to finish are apt to overlook needed revisions. Rewriting requires the sometimes arduous task of recopying or rekeying the product, a chore that some students prefer to avoid. Editing appears an overwhelming task to other students. Both the lack of practice and low expectations hamper many young writers. A final point to consider involves the sad thought that many students have never been taught how to revise their writing. They lack a basic plan to help them get started and then monitor the process. In addition to those who are disabled by teachers who do not teach the editing process, many types of special students require focused instruction as well as encouragement to revise their writings.

Implications.   The revision step is the point at which to present targeted lessons in grammar and mechanics. Teaching students to edit and rewrite assists them in becoming responsible for what they write and learning to improve both style and quality. With each revision, they learn more about how to write. Students are also apt to express their ideas more freely during the initial phases of writing because they do not worry about the mechanics at that point. Then, with the stress of generating ideas behind them, they can attend to the finer points of form, style, and mechanics as well as the use of clearer and more vivid language. Routinely revising written products is both a skill and a habit to be developed and nurtured.

CORRECTION Modify these strategies to meet students' learning needs.

1. *Editor's Checklist.* Give students guidelines to help them revise their writing:
    a. Could I easily outline my writing?
    b. Do I have a strong beginning and ending?
    c. Do my words and sentences make sense?
    d. Do any of my sentences sound out of place?
    e. Does each paragraph have a main idea?
    f. Do I use any words too often?
    g. Does my punctuation make it sound the way I say it?
    h. Have I capitalized the right words?
    i. Are the words spelled correctly?
    j. Is it legible and neat?

    As students become to accustomed to using a checklist, reduce the list to key terms or ideas (e.g., outline, spelling, organization, etc.). Develop a simplified checklist for younger and less able students.
2. *Teacher's Aide.* Ask students to be your editorial aide for the day. Think aloud as you consider possible changes in a brief composition. Next, talk your aide through similar revisions, supplying the verbal cues for points such as those listed in Activity 1. Then, have your aide think aloud the revisions. Finally, have the aide edit several papers of other students.
3. *Computer Proofwriting.* Word-processing programs can be ideal writing and editing tools. They free students to express their ideas, knowing that editing can be easily accomplished during revisions. After praising and discussing with students the content of their writing, read their compositions aloud to them. Guide them to explain, rearrange, and organize their ideas; combine, expand or reduce sentences; or add more picturesque terms. Then, have them read aloud their product, correcting punctuation, capitalization, and grammar as they read. Consider teaching the use of a companion spellchecker or editing program to assist the proofwriting.
4. *Personal Edits.* Guide students to develop their own checklists for revisions. Analyze with each student the areas in which he or she seldom needs revisions and the ones in which errors are frequent; then have students construct their personal editing lists that cite only the points most likely to need revisions. As skills improve, revise the checklists to reflect the progress.
5. *Proof Practice.* Provide copies of poorly written passages. Specify the number and types of errors that are present, but do not identify them. Have students read aloud each passage, correct and revise it, and then read it aloud again to check the "sound" of their revisions.
6. *Extra Practice.* • Pair students to alternate reading aloud compositions and suggesting revisions. • Have students write passages with errors for peers to correct, as in Proof Practice. • Occasionally make deliberate errors when writing and reward the students who notice.

49. SPELLING CORRECTLY ON TESTS

DETECTION This may be a special skill need of students who:

- Perform poorly on spelling tests
- Exhibit inconsistent spelling performance
- Spell better on weekly tests than on unit tests
- Are not good spellers in general (SN 50–51)
- Have weak word-recognition skills (SN 24–27)

Description. Correct spelling is a mechanical skill that supports written expression. Spelling words correctly on spelling tests is often easier than spelling words correctly on daily work. For weekly tests, one need only memorize a short list of words. For success, students must develop a study system and stay calm during the tests. Regular, teacher-directed practice sessions are very helpful for most students.

Causation. Some students have heard adults decry spelling as a difficult task and even state, "I (your father or your mother) couldn't spell either." Such statements almost give students permission to give up on spelling. Admittedly, spelling tests present a real problem for some students. Language differences, auditory discrimination or processing problems, or poor visual memory can make spelling tests high-anxiety experiences. Poor spelling test performance can also result from test anxiety, inadequate study habits, or some degree of linguistic dysfunction associated with phonics or decoding in general. Special groups of students who may exhibit spelling problems include the hearing impaired, language disabled, learning disabled, or speech disordered.

Implications. The most obvious implication of poor spelling is poor spelling grades. Many weak spellers also exhibit problems in the other language arts. Spelling skills can be taught along with related word-analysis skills. Structural analysis skills may offer particular assistance with multisyllabic words. Spelling interventions might involve simply reducing the number or types of words to be mastered for any one test, identifying a specific study method that works for specific students and then teaching it, or giving students extra practice sessions before tests.

CORRECTION Modify these strategies to meet students' learning needs.

1. *Sensations.* Have students experiencing serious problems trace words in sand or on sandpaper with their fingers. Using their fingers, guide students to either trace or spell, without the help of prelettered patterns, the target word and at the same time pronounce the word. If necessary, pronounce the word with the student. Some teachers also find it necessary to guide students' fingers until they learn to trace and pronounce words. Move from the use of more tactile writing materials to the chalkboard and then to tracing words on paper.
2. *Pretest Method.* Begin with a pretest containing new words. Immediately after completion of the pretest, have students check and correct their own papers to determine which words they need to study. Guide them to analyze their errors to determine why each error was probably made. Following instruction for 2–3 days, give a second test, but only include the words that were missed on the first test. Again, have students check, correct, explain errors, and receive credit for correct words. Repeat procedures until all words are spelled correctly. Retest students on the entire original list, and repeat the process as needed. When 90% of the words are spelled correctly, begin with a new list.
3. *Spelling Test Guidelines.* The following suggestions are intended to help students maximize their spelling test efforts:
    a. Learn the words that seem to be easiest first.
    b. Try to develop a visual image of how each word looks.
    c. Match each word with a similar word you already know to help you remember the new word.
    d. Use any unusual letter patterns to help remember words.
    e. Use pretend tests to prepare for spelling tests; be sure to take pretend tests in the same manner as the real ones.
    f. If words are very difficult, study only 1–2 at a time; rest 5 minutes, respell the first 1–2 words, and then add 1–2 more words, and repeat.
4. *Look, Say, and See.* Guide students to follow a 6-step procedure to study words: a) Look at the word; say it; see it in your mind; b) Copy the word; c) Look, say, and see; d) Write the word without looking; e) Check, look, say, see, and write; f) Write without looking.
5. *Spelling Update.* Teach a few words at a time, and check retention before presenting new words. Begin by teaching and testing a core of 3–5 words. Once a word is spelled correctly on 5 consecutive daily tests, drop that word and add a new one to the cycle.
6. *Extra Practice.* • Provide audiotapes of the next spelling test for students to hear and respond to on their own. • Use progress charts to encourage continued progress on spelling tests. • Help students form study groups to study for spelling tests. • Adapt ideas from Special Needs 24–26.

50. SPELLING CORRECTLY ON DAILY WORK

DETECTION This may be a special skill need of students who:

- Frequently misspell words on daily assignments
- Appear to be careless in how they spell
- Spell well on spelling tests but not on daily work
- Display poor handwriting to possibly hide spelling errors (SN 54)
- Have weak word-recognition skills (SN 24–27)
- Seldom use a dictionary voluntarily (SN 38)

Description. Spelling correctly on daily assignments is the intended goal of spelling lessons and tests; however, it is a much more difficult task than correct spellings on tests. Daily attention to spelling has been called an unending task similar to the dieter's daily need to be careful about what is eaten. One of the greatest dangers in allowing students to misspell words on daily work is that in a matter of days, the misspellings may look correct to them.

Causation. For many students, their misspelled words reflect carelessness, a lack of motivation, not being taught how to remember spellings, inadequate knowledge of proofreading and dictionary usage, a limited reading and speaking vocabulary, and difficulties associated with short- and long-term memory. Infrequent written expression experiences can hamper spelling. The excessive use of fill-in, circle, underline, and select-the-letter-of-the-best answer types of practice give student few opportunities to apply their spelling skills. When spelling is viewed as a test-only activity, daily spelling efforts are sometimes considered to be less important. Auditory and visual handicaps are responsible for some spelling problems. A number of special students, including some gifted youngsters who are not concerned with details, frequently misspell words in daily work.

Implications. The extent to which spelling problems interfere with students' performance and progress in all areas depends on their teachers' grading policies. Some teachers count misspelled words as incorrect responses, even on science tests; others grade only the content of the response. The most important words for students to learn to spell correctly are high-frequency words and key terms. A caution is appropriate in dealing with spelling on daily assignments: Excessive or repeated criticism about spelling can cause some students to stop writing. Spelling is an important literacy skill, but as adults, the students will probably have access to dictionaries or spelling checkers for correcting errors. Proofreading activities should, however, include analysis of spelling; proofwriting should follow. Be sure to use a positive manner in recognizing content and special efforts beyond the mechanics of spelling and grammar.

CORRECTION Modify these strategies to meet students' learning needs.

1. *Process Emphasis.* Process writing includes, among other steps, editing or proofwriting. Editing should become second nature and include a check for correct spelling on short-answer as well as sentence- and paragraph-length material. Use the chalkboard to demonstrate how to go through a paper and proofread for errors, particularly spelling. If word processors are available, permit the occasional use of spellcheckers.

2. *Careful Consideration.* Assist students to develop an attitude of careful thought about troublesome words. Guide students to a) pronounce words to themselves; b) lightly write their best guesses at the spellings of the words; c) look up the questionable words after they have finished writing; d) correct their errors; and e) record the questionable words on a personal list of troublesome words to which to refer. To avoid classroom interruptions, assign a spelling buddy to assist in the location process. Add or have students add the questionable words to their spelling list for the week. Good spelling is part habit and part attitude; requiring care and cooperation can help build the proper habits and attitudes.

3. *Dictionary Detection.* Demonstrate the utility of the dictionary for word spellings using the students' own words. If the dictionary seems to overwhelm students, use a picture or simplified dictionary. To begin practice, you may need to enforce somewhat unrealistic rules, such as requiring students to check the spelling of at least 3 words on a given assignment until they have established the habit. Permit the use of the spelling references during content tests, with the stipulation that spelling errors will be counted off; this is often sufficient motivation to encourage the use of such resources.

4. *Credited Spelling.* If necessary, award additional bonus points to students' spelling grades or award special privileges if spelling on daily work is maintained or improved throughout a specified time period. Contract the timelines and the reward with students who have particular difficulty.

5. *Troublesome Patterns.* Students sometimes display spelling difficulties associated with specific patterns of words. Explain recurring letter patterns, find and discuss related words, and include the pattern words in the individual student's weekly list until mastered.

6. *Troublesome Exceptions.* Teach students exceptions or words that seem to be spelled in a manner that is inconsistent with the language system. Underline the differences, clarify pronunciation, find words that follow a similar pattern, and have students pronounce and write the words. Have students who correctly spell the target words explain how they remember them; then refer back to these spelling demons regularly.

7. *Extra Practice.* • Develop author or proofreading teams of students for the purpose of looking over each others' work before considering an assignment finished. • Adapt ideas from Special Needs 24–26.

51. SPELLING SIMPLE AND COMMON WORDS

DETECTION This may be a special skill need of students who:

- Are poor spellers on tests and daily work (SN 49–50)
- Exhibit serious problems spelling
- Reveal inconsistent spelling patterns
- Appear to be trying but not improving their spelling
- Substitute unrelated words
- Demonstrate weak word-recognition skills (SN 24–27)

Description.   Correct spelling of common and high-frequency words is essential to functional literacy. These words occur so often that it is not practical for students to request assistance or consult a reference for each one. When students need help spelling simple words, you are faced with the task of providing personalized programming of a specific nature. Spelling involves several language abilities, any one of which can facilitate or impede students' spelling progress.

Causation.   Students who are unable to spell common words, despite repeated instruction and practice, usually have serious deficits that complicate their ability to learn. Many of these students also exhibit significant reading problems as well as poor performance in all the language arts. Both short- and long-term memory may be affected. These problems seem to involve an apparent inability to connect letters and sounds in a meaningful sense due to a lack of verbal recognition or language processing. Certain types of learning disabled students are also known for experiencing letter and word reversals, which can seriously impede their spelling achievement. It should be noted that in some cases, the problem is one of teaching, not learning; past instruction has simply been inappropriate to the student's learning needs.

Implications.   Teaching spelling through oral language is very difficult when working with students who are unable to spell the common and simple words. Although using dictated stories and having students copy their efforts can be used, more direct, structured spelling intervention will usually be required. In many cases, it is necessary to include language development along with auditory and visual intervention. You may need to offer corrective instruction for letter and sound discrimination tasks, visual discrimination, and perhaps a variety of speech tasks. Attention may also be needed in such areas as alphabetizing, letter formation, or handwriting. Some of the strategies appropriate for teaching letters, sight words, and phonics can be incorporated into a spelling program. Random instruction often results in more frustration than improved spelling performance. Instruction that focuses on diagnosed strengths is essential.

CORRECTION Modify these strategies to meet students' learning needs.

1. *Recognizing Spelling Errors.* The following list of major spelling errors may be used to help identify specific problem areas on which to focus instruction. There are other types of errors, but these are some of the most common: 1) phonetically correct; 2) letter reversals; 3) vowel substitutions; 4) vowel omissions; 5) consonant substitutions; and 6) consonant omissions.

2. *Personalization.* Most students with spelling problems need individual or small-group instruction. The use of personal chalkboards (plywood painted with two coats of chalkboard paint), manipulative letters on a flannel- or pegboard, and the use of magic markers, felttip pens, or brush and paint help maintain interest and make spelling a different learning experience.

3. *Multisensory Instruction.* Much like Sensations, in Special Need 49, the use of strategies that involve students in seeing, saying, touching, and moving letters can help reinforce spelling. The use of cut-out letters from tagboard or plastic moveable alphabets can help students assemble letters and gain a "feel" for each word. A few students may even benefit from having words traced on their back as they are tracing raised outlines of words with their fingers and spelling the word aloud. In most cases, only 1–2 words should be presented and studied in one 10–15-minute session. Begin the next session by reviewing the previous words; if they are not recalled, reteach them.

4. *Image Writing II.* Emphasize each step of the procedure suggested for remembering letters and sight words (Special Need 25). Write the target word on the board, placing above it a key picture, such as a red crayon for *red*. Students should a) use their index and middle fingers to trace each letter of the word you wrote while saying the letter names; b) copy the word underneath the stimulus, saying the letter names; c) repeat the tracing of the word you wrote, saying letters; d) copy and spell aloud again; and e) repeat steps c and d. After 3 tracings of the word you wrote, most of the chalk should be erased, leaving only the image of the markings. Have students close their eyes and try to see the word, and then trace the image with chalk, again spelling aloud. Erase the board and have students write the word from memory, repeating the procedures as needed.

5. *Look, Say, and See II.* Guide students to repeat a 6-step procedure several times to study words: a) Look at the word: say it; see it in your mind; b) Copy the word; say each letter as you write; c) Look, say, see, and trace and say the letters; d) Write the word without looking; e) Check, correct, look, say, see, and write and say; f) Write without looking and check.

6. *Extra Practice.* • Prepare easy word-search puzzles using spelling words. • Have students play Go Fish by spelling words on index cards. • Give students groups of 3 target spelling words; have them find the one in each group that is misspelled. • Adapt activities from Special Needs 24–27.

52. WRITING LEGIBLY ON HANDWRITING LESSONS

DETECTION This may be a special skill need of students who:

- Form letters incorrectly
- Write with an improper slant
- Hold their hand or pencil incorrectly when writing
- Write with lines too heavy, light, or inconsistent
- Write too quickly or too slowly
- Produce messy writing papers

Description. Handwriting, like spelling, is a mechanical skill that supports the other subject areas. It is the medium through which most students record their responses to school assignments. Both styles of handwriting are typically introduced during the first three grade levels. Manuscript writing, or printing, is usually taught in the first two grade levels; cursive, or "real" writing, is often introduced at the third-grade level. A combination of skills contribute to legible handwriting, including size, shape, slant, spacing, and proportion of letters and words. Although not generally considered a major or core subject, handwriting can facilitate or impede students' demonstration of content knowledge.

Causation. Perhaps the major cause of poor handwriting is poor teaching. In recent years, the emphasis on precise handwriting has decreased to the point that formal lessons occur infrequently in most classrooms. Many teachers do not use a standard format for their own writing, and a large majority have not been trained to teach children to write. Their attitudes of disinterest are conveyed to their students. Physical delays, visual motor weaknesses, and neurological dysfunctions, in addition to lack of appropriate instruction, can interfere with the ability to write legibly. Among the groups of special students who may experience difficulty writing legibly are the learning disabled, physically handicapped, and visually impaired. Impulsive and impatient students often write poorly, as do some of those who write with the left hand.

Implications. The obvious implication of illegible handwriting is poor grades in handwriting. However, the more important implication is the failure to master the mechanics for recording answers and responses in all subjects. Illegible responses are seldom acknowledged as correct.

CORRECTION Modify these strategies to meet students' learning needs.

1. *Trace and Write.* To teach letter formation, write each letter on the board. Have students trace over your letter several times and then copy it below your model. If their letters are less than perfect, superimpose the correct letter using colored chalk. Have students also trace with the colored chalk and then again copy the letter. Repeat until no chalk corrections are needed.

2. *Write and Trace.* Guide students to evaluate their own handwriting using transparent overlays. When a letter is incorrect, teach them to trace over it correctly in colored pen and then write it again. Begin by telling them the number of letters on the page that should be corrected, but do not specify which letters. Have them locate the errors with the overlay. Then demonstrate how to remove the overlay and superimpose the correct strokes with the colored pen.

3. *Tell and Write.* As you teach a letter, give verbal cues for each movement. Describe each stroke as you write at the board (e.g., "start, pull, dot" for lowercase *i*). Have students repeat the cues as you write additional examples. Next, have them say the strokes as they write the same letter at the board. Finally, have students tell the strokes as they write the letter on their papers.

4. *Disappearing Dots.* After introducing specific letters, make a dotted outline of the letter on the board. Mark with a tiny star or arrow the point at which to begin. Have students trace over the dots with chalk, moving from dot to dot until filling in the letter outline. Have them verbalize the strokes as they write. Then give them a page filled with the dotted outlines of the letters. The outlines on the first line should contain many dots spaced closely together. On the second line, the dots should be a little farther apart. Decrease the number of dots and increase the white spaces as you progress down the page until on the last line only the starting point is marked for students to write the letter without aid.

5. *Alternative Communications.* Some students may never be able to write legibly. Although you should make every effort to teach them to write their signature, consider teaching alternative means of communication. Teach keyboarding on a typewriter or computer. Permit the use of tape recorders or individual oral interviews by the teacher. Allow those students who write only with extreme effort to write the first few responses of each lesson and then answer orally or use the keyboard for the remaining responses.

6. *Extra Practice.* • Have students write target letters with their index fingers in wet sand or form letters from clay. • Allow pairs of students to take turns coaching each other to write, with one student supplying the verbal cues for the partner to follow and write. • Have pairs of students practice reading, spelling, and writing basic sight words. • Adapt strategies from Special Need 24.

53. WRITING LEGIBLY ON DAILY WORK

DETECTION This may be a special skill need of students who:

- Submit written assignments that are difficult to read
- Produce messy written work
- Appear careless in completing written assignments
- Seem to know more than their written responses indicate
- Dislike writing
- Alternate between manuscript and cursive writing

Description. Writing legibly on daily work is the intended goal of handwriting lessons. Daily handwriting involves the same basic elements of legibility as handwriting lessons: size, shape, slant, spacing, and proportion of letters and words. Personal styles, intensity, and consistency are also involved. The positions of the paper and the hand while writing not only influence the legibility but may also reflect the degree of effort that must be exerted for the individual students to write. The handwriting that is acceptable for daily assignments is typically more fluent and less exact than that expected on handwriting lessons. As students progress through the traditional curriculum, the demands for handwritten responses increase.

Causation. As previously noted, the primary cause of illegible handwriting is ineffective teaching. Students whose performance of handwriting lessons is unsatisfactory often perform even worse on daily writing tasks. Even those who are able to form their letters perfectly for special lessons may not do so when the focus is on the content of the written response, not on the mechanics of recording. Illegibility on daily assignments often results when the students' minds work faster than their hands, causing them to race through the writing in effort to keep up with their thoughts. This is particularly true of gifted, impatient, and impulsive youngsters. Physical delays, visual motor weaknesses, and neurological dysfunctions can interfere with the ability to write legibly. Among the groups of special students who may experience difficulty writing legibly are the learning disabled, physically handicapped, and visually impaired.

Implications. Students whose writing is not clearly legible often receive low grades in all subjects. In effect, they are graded on their writing problems, not on their knowledge of the subjects about which they write. Because many poor writers record responses only with great effort, they often write a fraction of what they know or do not finish assignments. It is important for teachers to view handwriting as a tool for expressing thoughts and knowledge. When that tool impedes expression, substitute alternatives such as keyboarding, a valuable tool for improving written expression of all types.

CORRECTION Modify these strategies to meet students' learning needs.

1. *Writing Grader.* As a matter of principle, award 2 grades to each written assignment: 1 for the content of the students' responses and 1 for the handwriting. If work is not neat and legible, return it to students. Have them correct their own handwriting using a colored felttip pen to write over their errors. If that does not increase legibility, then have them rewrite the assignment for their writing grade. This strategy rewards those who write correctly the first time and motivates those who do not to improve so that they do not have to rewrite assignments.

2. *Twice Write.* Guide students who have writing difficulties to record their responses first as a rough draft that they can read. Then have them use a word processor or typewriter to produce a final copy that you can read. Using this format, the first writing is the one that expresses ideas while the second one is an alternative handwriting exercise.

3. *Target Instruction.* Some students need specific instruction in only 1–2 of the major handwriting elements. In these cases, place a student's hand in yours as you write together or have students watch your model and join in as you describe strokes and form words. If a few quick lessons do not remedy the problem, conduct formal handwriting lessons (Special Need 52).

4. *Contracted Writing.* When students seem to know more than their written responses indicate, implement a writing contract. First, orally quiz the students to determine the extent of the gap between what they know and what they write; discuss the problem with them. Then, agree on a certain proportion of each assignment to be handwritten legibly, with a greater portion to be keyboarded. The particular ratios that are reasonable depend on the degree to which handwriting problems interfere with expression. For a student with mild problems, the contract might be for the first half of each assignment to be handwritten and the last half keyboarded; a more serious problem might require only the first paragraph to be handwritten. A complex problem might even call for most responses to be given orally.

5. *Meaning and Reason.* The handwriting required for daily work should be both meaningful and reasonable. Writing a new story ending is more meaningful than copying the whole story. What is a reasonable amount of writing and amount of time in which to accomplish it will vary according to students' handwriting proficiency; writing contracts can make the demands more reasonable for individual students. Practices such as punishing students by having them copy pages from an encyclopedia and write repeated "I shall not" lines are neither meaningful nor reasonable but instead are almost guaranteed to teach negative handwriting habits and attitudes.

6. *Extra Practice.* • Encourage neatness by displaying daily spotlight papers that are written neatly and legibly. • Use individual chalkboards for students to practice their written responses. • Adapt strategies from Special Need 52.

54. WRITING FLEXIBILITY

DETECTION This may be a special skill need of students who:

- Do not vary writing speed according to the task
- Exert the same amount of effort for every writing task
- Attempt to use one style or type of writing for all purposes
- Use inappropriate letter size for space available
- Have not fully mastered manuscript and cursive writing (SN 52–53)

Description.   Handwriting flexibility requires students to judge the form their writing should take and the speed and care with which they should write. In order to do this, students must have developed the most basic of the writing skills. Completing an application, signing a library card, addressing a letter, responding to a test question, taking a phone message, taking notes in class, or printing a notice all require varied types, styles, and speeds of writing. Much as students must vary their reading rate according to the type and purpose for reading, they must also adjust their writing to fit the type and purpose for writing.

Causation.   Inflexible handwriting results from inflexible instruction and inadequate mastery of the handwriting skills. Many students, particularly young or special ones, do not realize that different writing tasks require different writing styles and may even become easier when specific forms of handwriting are used. Often this is because their teachers have insisted that they always "Write their very best," which translates to students as "Draw your letters perfectly." Some teachers fail to expose students to and involve them in a varied program of handwriting for different purposes. Students who have difficulty with or are uncertain of their handwriting skills tend to stick to the form and style with which they are the most comfortable. Finally, some students exhibit poor fluency due to problems involving limited perceptual motor skills or coordination difficulties that physically inhibit their ability to substantially adjust handwriting rate, style, and proportions.

Implications.   Handwriting flexibility results from the integration of the mastery of many skills. This collection of skills allows students to decide how to select the particular form or written format that is appropriate for each task. However, students must be taught various formats and then provided meaningful practice using each. Many students are relieved to discover that on some occasions, it is permissible and even advisable to write quickly and not too perfectly. Unless they master writing flexibility, students will be limited in the options they have as they encounter different tasks that demand different types of writing.

CORRECTION Modify these strategies to meet students' learning needs.

1. *3-Speed Writes.* Teach students 3 types and speeds of writing. Introduce the first speed, "Slow," during a handwriting lesson. Discuss the other purposes of writing slowly and forming letters carefully, such as when writing a letter to someone they want to impress. Then, whenever you want students to demonstrate their best handwriting, tell them to use their "slow" writing. Introduce the second writing speed, "Flow," as the most useful one that they will use for the majority of the writing tasks, both in and out of school. Explain that this is the smooth, easy writing that feels comfortable to the writer and is reasonably legible to the reader. Remind students to use their "flow" writing for most daily assignments. Introduce the third writing speed, "Go," with a competitive game in which students race to write answers quickly. Discuss the other uses of "go" writing, such as taking phone messages and taking notes in class. Later, in class, when you want students to write fast, tell them to use their "go" writing. The 3 terms are important verbal cues to guide students to vary their writing according to the task.

2. *Writing Rhythm.* To demonstrate the rhythm of fluent handwriting, have students listen to music and write to the rhythm. Select music to match each of the writing speeds of Activity 1. Begin with "slow" and have students write carefully to the rhythm of slow music and then discuss the purposes of this writing speed. Follow a similar procedure for "go" writing to the rhythm of fast music and then music of moderate tempo for "flow" writing. Experiment with several moderate tempos until students find their best fluid speed that also results in reasonably legible handwriting.

3. *Handwriting Sampler.* Use samples of students' handwriting to illustrate the different types of handwriting that are used for certain situations. Construct a poster to leave on display in the classroom. Head the left column with "Purpose" and list types of documents or situations (e.g., sign, personal note, phone message, handwriting lessons). For the middle column, write "Speed" to indicate which of the 3 speeds is most appropriate for the particular purpose. Entitle the right column "Sample" and show 1–3 examples of students' handwriting that represent each category in the first column. Refer to the sampler as you assign writing tasks.

4. *Handwriting Checklist.* Post a handwriting checklist showing students' handwriting progress. Beside each name, check desirable features as they are mastered. In addition to adjusting writing speed, include size, slant, and proper spacing as well as letter formation, neatness, and posture.

5. *Extra Practice.* • Highlight 1 form of handwriting every few weeks; list 2–3 situations for students to use as they look at your sample and try to write their own responses using an appropriate style. • Provide samples of writing that are not appropriate as they exist; have students work in pairs to discuss what they think is wrong and then rewrite each sample correctly.

55. WRITING LEFT-HANDED

DETECTION This may be a special skill need of students who:

- Experience difficulty writing legibly and neatly
- Hook the left hand to write
- Hold the paper inappropriately for left-handed writing
- Slant letters incorrectly
- Have difficulty spacing letters and words
- Tire easily when writing
- Grip the pencil incorrectly
- Demonstrate poor posture when writing

Description. Estimates of the number of left-handed students range from 5–10% of the school population, the average representing a few more males than females. As reflected in the number and nature of observed difficulties, left-handed students frequently experience problems learning to write. Their problems often tend to be of a more serious nature than those of right-handed students. When they write, their body language often speaks of awkwardness and intense effort.

Causation. Many of the difficulties experienced by left-handed students result from trying to adjust to a right-handed world. Some right-handed teachers actually create handwriting problems for these students. The writing models and directions that are appropriate for most students are inappropriate and often counterproductive for left-handed students. The use of right-handed desks makes writing more difficult. Left-to-right motions are particularly awkward for left-handed students. When writing with the right hand, the left-to-right movement permits a constant view of both what is being written at the moment and what has just been written. However, when writing with the left hand, it is difficult to watch as letters are formed and the writing hand partially obstructs the view of what has just been written. This interferes with self-monitoring and spacing and encourages the hooked hand, twisted neck or shoulder positions, and poor posture so characteristic of these students. The poor postures in turn complicate the writing task. A disproportionate number of students with various special needs are also left handed.

Implications. Before age 8, students who exhibit no clear preference should be encouraged to use their right hand, since school, work, and social conditions are generally intended for right-handed individuals. Once a preference for using the left hand for writing has been established, there is no justification for forcing a change to the right. Left-handed students must be taught left-handed strategies for handwriting, including paper position, slant, posture, and demonstrations of letter formation. Instruction may need to be not only more specific but also more intense.

CORRECTION Modify these strategies to meet students' learning needs.

1. *Chalk Talks.* The exaggerated arm movements that are required to write on the chalkboard illustrate and reinforce the proper motions for writing. Introduce the basic component strokes of letters—such as circles, curves, and vertical, horizontal, and slanted lines—or the letters themselves at the chalkboard, verbalizing the strokes. Have students say the strokes as you demonstrate. Guide them to trace your model as they describe the strokes. Emphasize the motions as they make them. Contrary to right-handed instruction, a vertical or left slant is acceptable. Providing practice using exaggerated arm movements often makes it easier for left-handed students to develop proper motion and slant. Note that the hand does not obscure the writing. As students consistently demonstrate mastery of a letter or stroke, have them write it on their papers, verbalizing the strokes. If hand, paper, or body position are incorrect or letters are poorly formed, have students return to the board and repeat the procedures.

2. *Paper Placement.* Proper paper placement is critical to the left-handed writer. The paper should be placed on a 30-degree angle, turned clockwise, and placed slightly off center to the left side of the desk. This is the opposite of the placement for a right-handed writer. If possible, the desk or writing table for a left-handed student should be slightly lower to allow the students to more easily view their work.

3. *Left-Hand Pencils.* A hard lead pencil should be used, since the lead will not break or smear easily. Some students grip their pencils so tightly and bear down so hard that they constantly break the lead. Many of these students tend to move their hand and arm over their work and sometimes smudge their writing. Holding the pencil 1 or 1-1/2 inches from the point helps students see what they are doing. The writing instrument should be slanted with the blunt end toward the student's left shoulder. Special pencil grips and shaped pencils are designed to encourage correct pencil grip. If these are not available, wrap a rubber band around the pencil as a grip.

4. *Model Mentors.* Seat left-handed students together as an instructional group. Then find a left-handed teacher or older student who has already developed satisfactory handwriting skills. Invite him or her to your class to work with your left-handed group. The students will enjoy seeing that a left-handed person can write well and will probably gain a few hints for adjusting to a right-handed world. If no mentor is available and you are a right-handed teacher, practice writing with your left until you can demonstrate the movements in the air and then on the chalkboard.

5. *Extra Practice.* • Provide personal chalkboards for independent practice. • Provide center activities for drawing, tracing, and clay modeling to improve eye-hand coordination. • Display charts showing hand and pencil position for left-handed writing. • Adapt ideas from Special Needs 52—54.

REFLECTIONS

1. The introduction to Part V presents a general overview of writing skills. Review this section and then go back and skim the introductions to the previous three sections. Compare the curricular role of writing to that of the other language arts. How would you explain the contention that as a nation, our students' writing skills are deficient? Which specific skills do you think create the most difficulty? Why?

2. Part V is organized according to four major skill areas of writing: written expression, written grammar, spelling, and handwriting. Compare the skills listed in each area with the ones outlined in the scope and sequence charts for a major language text. Which areas receive the most attention? Do the skill listings vary according to grade level? Why? Which ones should receive more emphasis for special learners? Justify your responses.

3. Listed at the beginning of the discussion of each writing skill are some of the observable behaviors that signal problems in that skill. Select one of the four areas to observe in a regular and/or special classroom. During a specific writing or content lesson, observe to compare students' writing behaviors with the DETECTION behaviors listed for each of the skills in the chosen area. Note any other detective behaviors that you observe. Discuss the implications of these behaviors with experienced teachers.

4. When focused on a particular student with special writing needs, classroom observations often reveal important diagnostic and prescriptive data. Observe such a student in the classroom during writing instruction; compare observed behaviors with the DETECTION behaviors listed in this section for each special writing need. List your tentative conclusions and any additional information you need to confirm your hypotheses. If possible, repeat the observations of the same student on several occasions to compare progress.

5. For each special writing need, only a few CORRECTION strategies are listed. Based on your classroom observations and/or your own experience, add to or modify the corrective strategies for the special writing need of your choice.

6. Spelling and handwriting are presented as skills that support written expression. With this in mind, critique the suggestion that special students be permitted to use resources for spelling correctly on written assignments. What about all students? What is your position on permitting all students to substitute typewritten or word-processed work for handwritten assignments? Does it differ for handicapped students? Why or why not?

7. Many young students can freely express their ideas orally. Yet these same students are later unable to express their ideas in writing. Based upon your own experiences in school, identify the factors that impede and facilitate written expression. Then, translate these factors into instructional implications for teaching written expression to special students.

8. Planning targeted writing instruction for special learners often begins with careful observations of their behaviors while they are writing and analyses of their written products. Observe a special learner to identify his or her writing needs; then use the CORRECTIVE PRINCIPLES (Part I) to select and modify CORRECTION strategies to plan two writing lessons.

9. The appropriateness of corrective writing lessons for special learners is often easily discerned by analyzing the student's written products before and after lessons. Implement your writing plans to teach two writing lessons to a special learner; then compare the student's writing to previous written work.

10. Suggestions for teaching special students to write are presented in several language arts and special education references. Compare and contrast discussions in these sources with the information in Chapters 12–15:

Choate, J. S., Bennett, T. Z., Enright, B. E., Miller, L. J., Poteet, J. A., & Rakes, T. A. (1987). *Assessing and programming basic curriculum skills.* Boston: Allyn and Bacon.

Graham, S. & Harris, K. R. (Guest Eds.). (1988). Research and instruction in written language [Special issue]. *Exceptional Children,* 54 (6), 491–584.

Hall, J. K. (1986). *Evaluating and improving written expression: A practical guide for teachers (2nd ed.).* Boston: Allyn and Bacon.

Hasenstab, M. S., & Laughton, J. (1982). *Reading, writing, and the exceptional child.* Rockville, MD: Aspen.

Henderson, E. (1985). *Teaching spelling.* Boston: Houghton Mifflin.

Hennings, D. G. (1986). *Communication in action: Teaching the kanguage arts* (3rd ed.). Boston: Houghton Mifflin.

Mann, P. H., Suiter, P. A., & McClung, R. M. (1987). *Handbook in diagnostic-prescriptive teaching* (3rd ed.). Boston: Allyn and Bacon.

Norton, D. E. (1987). *The effective teaching of language arts* (2nd ed.). Columbus, OH: Charles E. Merrill.

Rico, G. L. (1983). *Writing the natural way.* Los Angeles: J.P. Tarcher.

Stoodt, B. D. (1988). *Teaching language arts.* New York: Harper and Row.

Temple, C., Nathan, R., Burris, N, & Temple, F. (1988). *The beginnings of writing* (2nd ed.). Boston: Allyn and Bacon.

Wallace, G., Cohen, S. B., & Polloway, E. A. (1987). *Language arts: Teaching exceptional students.* Austin, TX: Pro-Ed.

Index

ABOUT THE AUTHORS

THOMAS A. RAKES has two decades of experience as an educator, researcher, author, and consultant. He holds the Ed.D. from the University of Tennessee and is presently Professor of Education in the Department of Curriculum & Instruction at Memphis State University. In addition to the graduate and undergraduate courses he teaches in language arts, reading, assessment, content, and research, his experiences have included directing a university diagnostic center and teaching at the middle school, secondary school, and adult education levels. A prolific writer, he is the author of more than 80 articles in the areas of language arts, diagnostic/prescriptive instruction, and reading. His is co-author of *Reading: Detecting and Correcting Special Needs* (1989), *Assessing and Programming Basic Curriculum Skills* (Allyn and Bacon, 1987), two reading diagnosis texts, and a series of worktexts. Dr. Rakes has presented papers at numerous national and state conferences, and has been a consultant for school districts, colleges, and businesses in 41 states. He is on the advisory board for a major basal reading series and has been on the editorial board for several professional journals.

JOYCE S. CHOATE is Consulting Editor for the *Allyn and Bacon Detecting and Correcting Series*. She holds the Ed.D. from Memphis State University and is presently Professor of Special Education and Reading at Northeast Louisiana University. Her extensive teaching experiences have ranged from the preschool to the graduate levels in both regular and special education. She has also been an educational diagnostician and reading specialist. In addition to editing the four books in this series, she is co-author of *Reading: Detecting and Correcting Special Needs* (1989), *Assessing and Programming Basic Curriculum Skills* (Allyn and Bacon, 1987), and texts on reading diagnosis, gifted, and prescriptive teaching. She has presented numerous papers on assessment, prescriptive teaching, and reading at state and national conferences. Dr. Choate is presently Publications Chair of the Council for Educational Diagnostic Services (CEDS), and former President, and is an associate editor of *Diagnostique* and field editor of *Teaching Exceptional Children*.

READER'S REACTION

Dear Reader:

No one knows better than you the special needs of your students or the exact nature of your classroom problems. Your analysis of the extent to which this book meets *your* special needs will help us revise and improve this book, and assist us in developing other books in the *Allyn and Bacon Detecting and Correcting Series.*

Please take a few minutes to respond to the questionnaire on the next page. If you would like to receive a reply to your comments or additional information about the series, indicate this preference in your answer to the last question. Mail the completed form to:

> Joyce S. Choate, Consulting Editor
> Detecting and Correcting Series
> c/o Allyn and Bacon, Inc.
> 160 Gould Street
> Needham Heights, Massachusetts 02194-2310

Thank you for sharing your special needs and professional concerns.

Sincerely,

Joyce S. Choate

Joyce S. Choate

READER'S REACTION TO

Language Arts: Detecting and Correcting Special Needs

Name: _____   Position: _____

Address: _____   _____

_____   Date: _____

1. How have you used this book?

    ___College Text   ___Inservice Training   ___Teaching Resource

Describe:_____

2. For which purpose(s) do you recommend its use?

3. What do you view as the major strengths of the book?

4. What are its major weaknesses?

5. How could the book be improved?

6. What additional topics should be included in this book?

7. In addition to the books currently included in the *Allyn and Bacon Detecting and Correcting Series*—Basic Mathematics, Classroom Behavior, Language Arts, and Reading—what other books would you recommend developing?

8. Would you like to receive these items?

    ___A reply to your comments

    ___Additional information about this series

Additional Comments:

THANK YOU FOR SHARING YOUR SPECIAL NEEDS AND PROFESSIONAL CONCERNS